PASSING THE BATON:
Linking the Generations

A BIBLICAL LOOK AT MENTORING

PASSING THE BATON:
Linking the Generations

A BIBLICAL LOOK AT MENTORING

CAROLYN ROS

YWAM PUBLISHING
Seattle, Washington

Passing the Baton: Linking the Generations by Carolyn Ros

Original Dutch title: De verbinding tussen generaties
– Een bijbelse visie op mentorschap by Carolyn Ros
(ISBN 978-94-64250-24-4, e-book ISBN 978-94-64250-31-2)

Published in English with permission
by YWAM Publishing
a ministry of Youth With A Mission
P.O. Box 55787, Seattle, WA 98155-0787

For orders contact: www.ywampublishing.com or call (800) 922-2143

First printing 2023

ISBN 978-1-64836-127-2

Printed in the United states of America

Table of content

Preface		7
I	Introduction	11
II	Explanation of the title	15
III	What is mentoring	17
IV	Hope redefined: my back story	21
V	How to build a firm foundation	45
VI	Mentors who have shaped me	65
VII	Biblical examples of mentorship	77
VIII	A biblical framework for mentoring	93
IX	How to start	97
X	Qualities of a good mentor	109
XI	Skills of a good mentor	115
XII	Word of caution	121
XIII	Mentee: where to begin	125
XIV	Conclusion	129

Preface

The difference between a good story and a PR stunt is the lasting quality of what is being shared. A good story is always a good one, even when no one reads it. A PR stunt will only be successful when it pleases the masses. I recently read this and it put into words what I always had in mind about my life: I don't want my life to be a PR stunt, in the sense that it will only be successful when people think I am wonderful. I want my life to be a story that is worthwhile, even if nobody would read it.

Life is an art, also when I could not yet put it into words and I knew that I would need help to live it out. Every day we are bombarded with successful PR stunts and before you know it you start to imitate it.

So when I was 27 years old I made a wish list of things I would like to see in a spiritual mother.

It had to be someone I respected because of the way she lived her life. A wise woman who I could not intimidate with my words. God knows me better than I know myself. I was looking for someone who had walked a tough road, but is still gracious, witty and beautiful.

One year later I sat at a table with Carolyn Ros. After that meeting I went home and I had to cry because she was the exact person I had in mind. Now, four years after that first encounter, I still sit at her table and she sits at mine.

I don't think it is a requirement to be verbally strong, marked by life, gracious, witty and beautiful to be a mentor. I see this as a little joke from God, Who does not always literally answer my prayers, actually no rather than yes; that's why I assumed He thought I could use some wisdom and guidance in my life.

Something like: 'This is so important and if you want Me to provide in your excessive list of demands you will no longer have an excuse to live an orphaned life.'

I honestly believe that the other demands on my list are important for a mentor: that your life compels respect, more than words can do, that you are wise and know God.

When I met with Carolyn I did not really know what to expect. Did I need to give her weekly updates of my life? Or send her prayer requests? Ask her how she was doing? Underneath it all was another of my questions: What does she expect from me? Is it okay what I am doing? As time passes by I understand that she does not require that I perform. I am not her spiritual mother, it is the other way around. Perhaps the best way to explain this is that she often approaches me. How are you doing, dear heart? Shall we make an appointment? She keeps it very simple, but intentional. This gives me room to discover how I want to be someone's spiritual daughter.

And I think I am not the only one. I see many women around me – in their twenties and thirties – who apparently have an easy life, but they do sense that their life is slowly turning into a PR stunt. We all want a life worth living. The world needs to become a better place for those who come after us. Here are some examples that can be hard: How to relate to our Maker. To be single. To be married. To have a job or not. To be a mom or not. To prioritize. To pray. To build relationships or lose them. To be a family, or to miss one. To belong to a church, or to leave a church. To deal with sickness, trauma, disappointment.

But we need shoulders to stand on, someone who has trodden the grass on a path unknown to us. Somebody we trust to cheer us on, or corrects us. Also, we need to learn to ask for help more often.

I believe Carolyn is not the only one who is happy to lend a shoulder or trod the grass for someone to follow, or to live a life that is worthy to be trusted either in correction or in encouragement. Maybe those people still need to learn to reach out to the people who really need this.

Let this book be a guide to help you take the steps that you need to take without hesitation. Let it be a story that helps bring people together who have been waiting to find a mentor or be a mentor.

Rinke Verkerk
Journalist

I Introduction

Sitting at my desk, I was aroused out of my concentration by the ringing of my phone. A rather shy voice greeted me, but what I heard was courage. Courage to call and ask to meet up. Courage to acknowledge that life experiences need to be processed in order to make sense of the bigger storyline of life. Courage and boldness are needed to approach an older person. This softened my heart as I was listening with a willing spirit. Willingness in my heart to acknowledge how brave the other person was to reach out to me. And while listening to the person speaking, I tuned in to what the Holy Spirit wanted me to hear and how He wanted me to respond. The initial request was simple, 'can we meet for coffee?' I knew that this could be the first step in an adventure, maybe just for one coffee-moment, but also realizing that it could lead to many more moments of listening, evaluating, imparting and letting go. I was determined in my heart to acknowledge the courage that it takes for someone to take this first step. After the initial contact, the Holy Spirit would make it clear what the process would be.

'Many people in my generation lack spiritual parents. My own parents were not able to do this and this left a void in my young adulthood. Our times together helped me to stay on track spiritually. You gave motherly/fatherly advice without being emotionally clouded by being the real parent. Thank you for setting the standard and taking the time to walk alongside of me. You modelled the love of Jesus and discipleship so well. I want to mentor others the way I have been mentored.' —A Mentee

'My generation is in desperate need of spiritual moms and dads.' —A Mentee

There is a cry for 'spiritual parents' to come alongside of young believers to empower and equip them in their growth process. There is a need for restoration between the generations. We live in a time where fractured families have cheated the subsequent generations of experiencing authentic, anchored, committed relationships. Each person needs to be noticed and validated in order to build a healthy sense of self-worth and significance. Training and modelling need to take place to enable young people to grow in confidence in their responsibilities and achievements, knowing that someone believes that they have what it takes to succeed. The question remains whether or not the subsequent generations can learn how to work together. A tremendous blessing is released when each generation intentionally helps the next one to discover their God-given identity and purpose in life.

This process is not about helping build one's clientele or increasing one's name recognition. We have relegated compassion and care to the professionals when maybe all that is needed is a shoulder to lean on; a cup of tea and time; a listening ear and a listening heart; someone to be available to be a sounding board. Mentoring is a pay-it-forward model of enabling and equipping others on their journey of growth. So much of our society is based on the premise of: 'what do I get out of this?' 'What advantage does it give me?' 'Why would I invest time and energy in someone without being paid for it?' In the ensuing chapters, I hope to address some of these issues. I will also be sharing some of the 'pearls of wisdom' that I have been accumulating along the way. My prayer is that this will be a voyage of discovery of the enormous blessing that is released when the generations work together. No monetary amount can be attached to seeing the next generation take steps of faith, steps of courage, steps of hope.

II Explanation of the title

Life is like a relay-race.

A relay race is an event where a team of four athletes run equal predetermined distances in a sprint race, each passing a rod-like object called the 'baton' to the next person to continue the race. The strategy is to create a team of the fastest runners. The success of the team depends on each one doing their part. The team of athletes are interconnected and reliant upon the skills of the previous runner. Each runner must be prepared to pass the baton on to the next one in line, while continuing to run after the baton has been passed on.

The interaction of 'passing on' and 'receiving' the baton serve as an illustration of how one generation is poised to pass on to the next valuable life principles. This requires a certain rhythm , a certain dance in life. It requires agility, training, endurance, clarity of purpose and vision. It requires an understanding of how a team works and how generations thrive when they are interconnected. In the race, each athlete is facing forward, running into the future. Mentoring others is a valuable way of how each generation has something to pass on to the next. It is not about who is the strongest or most successful as the victory belongs to the whole team.

The Bible calls us to fulfill this mandate:

Ephesians 4:12 'Equipping the saints for the work of service to the building up of the Body of Christ.'

2 Timothy 2:2 'The things which you have heard from me in the presence of many witnesses, entrust these to faithful men who will be able to teach others also.'

III What is mentoring?

'I really appreciated the time you took to mentor me. You saw my potential and calling. You were patient and used encouraging words. Sharing your own life experiences helped me to hear God better for myself. You gave such compassionate input that was very life giving and authentic. You are not quick to judge or try to give the right solutions. You do not tell people what they should do but you walk along side of them. You provide a shoulder to lean on which gave a safe place to share my fears and my questions. Together we could look for answers.' —A Mentee

Mentoring is God's tool to develop disciples. As a noun, a mentor is an experienced and trusted advisor. As a verb it means 'to advise' or 'to train'. This is a voluntary relational process between a more mature, knowledgeable, skilled person and one who is eager to learn in an intentional way. Maturity is not age-related. In this relational process one person empowers the other by transferring his/her resources of insight, values and connection to the other.

> *We wanted a mentor to ask us the tough questions that we would not ask ourselves. We can accomplish much together with the Holy Spirit but sometimes we need an outside perspective to help shine light on our weak areas. We also wanted a place where we could come without questions and get another perspective, be challenged so that we could work things out together.'* —A Mentee

Every Christian who is serious about his/her faith should be involved in this process of both mentoring and being mentored. Growth happens when we invite others into our journey and also come alongside others on their journey. This process can be compared to a lake that is thriving with vegetation and fish because of the flow of fresh water coming into the lake and also flowing out of the lake. A lake with only input but no output will soon become stagnant.

> *'It is healthy for everyone to have a mentor. These are people who help you reflect and process the things that have happened. It is also helpful to share my struggles and receive wisdom.'* —A Mentee

The purpose of spiritual mentoring is to enhance one's relationship with God. It will also help the mentee to recognize how God is already at work in his/her life. This offers the opportunity to grow in character while having a sounding board to deal with some habits or challenges that one wants to see changed in one's life.

IV Hope redefined: my back story

'I chose you because I know a bit of your story. Your past circumstances and the way you share about them today is so full of hope, endurance and character. Your life and walk with the Lord is a huge testimony. Your wisdom comes from many long hard years of trusting in the Lord. This has made you a safe person to share with. You have faced challenges and this made me feel understood by you. I knew you would keep things in confidence and would remain neutral in the face of challenges. You showed care and love through all of the ups and downs.' —A Mentee

'You provide a safe place to process thoughts, fears, desires, past and present experiences. You gave a safe place to cry, share, feel, doubt and come to a place of joy and laughter. You provided a safe place because you shared your own experiences and struggles. This made you more authentic and not coming from a place of a teacher. You

> *gave equality in our conversation, I met the love of Christ as we talked. You listen well and give feedback when needed but you left space to share my thoughts. I felt love and not condemnation or that you tried to put your opinion on me. You gave me space to find answers for myself and sent me home with words of affirmation. You were patient to give space and time to process. We always closed our time with prayer, inviting the Holy Spirit to work in the situations that I was facing and trusting that He would speak to me. This gave hope and confidence in speaking together that God was at work. Our talks gave me a deeper understanding of God and my faith in Him, This makes me long for more of Him in my life. Your lifestyle of how you have handled past and present experiences is an example of faith in my life.'* —A Mentee

> Psalm 27:13 'I would have despaired unless I had believed to see the goodness of the LORD in the land of the living.'

The fasten-seatbelt sign was turned off and the frantic chaos erupted of tired passengers trying to retrieve their belongings from the overhead compartment. Excitement and trepidation filled my heart as I gathered the diaper bag and belongings for my 14 month old son. My strong husband was able to wrestle our carry-on bags from the overhead compartment.

The autumn weather welcomed us after we cleared customs at the International Airport Schiphol, near Amsterdam in the Netherlands

The year was 1975.

Our individual journeys had started some years before when we both left our homeland for further study and training in the UK. Our paths diverged after our studies and then reunited again after we had had a lengthy time of correspondence which had grown our hearts closer to each other. This was the type of growth where we knew beyond a shadow of a doubt that life would be better if we shared it together.

Our destiny was sealed in an unusual way. I had spent the first 18 years of my life in Japan, as the daughter of an American/Norwegian missionary couple. It had been my childhood desire to be married in that country and surrounded by the people that I knew and loved.

Four ceremonies were needed to tie-the-knot. My husband-to-be is Dutch which meant that our first ceremony was held at the Dutch Consulate in Kobe, Japan, followed by a ceremony at the American Consulate. The Japanese City Hall added enough paperwork to make our union binding whilst in that country.

My Dad officiated the church celebration followed by a reception that my Mom coordinated.

Our two-year visa allowed us to teach English to University students, eager business executives with ambitions to have their companies branch out beyond the confines of their island homeland and to children at a language institute.

A year after our marriage, our lives were enriched with the arrival of our oldest son. He was a small little miracle that launched us on the life-long journey called 'parenthood'.

Six weeks after Jozua's birth, we noticed bruises on his hands and legs. We weren't immediately concerned but the first hospital check-up quickly brought us some answers. Answers, however, that would turn our world upside-down.

The lab report came back with news that Jozua only had 12% coagulation in his blood. By this time, he was bleeding from his palate from nursing.

Life is so fragile, yet there is a tenacious longing to hold on, come what may.

After work, Johan joined me at the hospital. We were numb with shock and fear. As much as we wanted our baby to live, we prayed a very hard prayer. Through our tears, we relinquished him into the hands of Jesus. We so wanted to hold on to him, but we said: ' Jesus, You gave him life and his life is in Your hands.'

Jozua was admitted to hospital and placed in a ward with other babies with terminal illnesses while the doctors tried to decide if there was anything that they could possibly do. We were able to stay in a guest-house close by so that I could continue to nurse.

During the first night, both Johan and I suddenly sat up in bed with a sense of urgency to pray for our son's healing. Library shelves are filled with books on this subject, but when you see that your own baby is dying, the question remained, how do we really pray?

We asked the Holy Spirit to help us pray. He taught us a very significant and profound prayer: 'Lord, help.' Although the words were simple, they were accompanied by faith. There was a sense that something beyond our capacity to understand was taking place.

Throughout the course of the following day, I noticed that there were no new bruises and the old ones were already turning yellow, which is a sign of healing. When the doctors came back on duty after the weekend, all the blood tests were repeated. This time, however, the results showed 100% coagulation.

We were overjoyed and told the doctors that we had prayed to the God of the Bible. They were baffled and explained that they could not take credit for any of this as the blood plasma for Jozua's rare blood-type, that had been ordered from the international blood bank, had not yet arrived.

This occurrence marked our lives in an indelible way. Theories about God were becoming a deeper reality.

God hears.

God heals.

God saves.

God restores.

God redeems.

God gives hope.

Several years after our arrival in Japan our visa's had to be renewed. Our journey of faith had been challenged and grown significantly through Jozua's healing. We boldly asked the Lord, in prayer, what our next step should be. Should we stay where we were in Japan where I was raised? Should we go to the Netherlands where Johan was born and raised? Should we go the States where I was born?

During our prayer time, God encouraged us with a word that we received as a promise.

This word was: ' The LORD is going to pour out His Spirit over the Netherlands and Europe and that He wanted to prepare us for that.'

Having seen our son restored to health was enough proof for us to pack our bags and embark on the long journey to the Netherlands.

After clearing customs, Johan's uncle brought us to Johan's hometown close to Rotterdam.

During the ensuing weeks we reconnected with his church. We shared about our journey of the previous years and the promise that had brought us to the Netherlands.

We quickly discovered that there was not much acceptance or belief in what we shared.

Had we just imaged this promise? Had God really spoken? Or had we just made the biggest mistake of our lives?

In desperation, we went back to the LORD in prayer. What was His timing? What was our assignment? Was He really going to fulfil what He had promised? How would we recognize the promise when it came? How did He want us to respond when criticism came our way? How should we deal with disappointment and delays?

We took several weeks to pray and fast. During this time, a verse came to mind that helped give some clarity.

Psalm 37:3 ' Dwell in the land and cultivate faithfulness.'

This was not a verse for one with a tourist mentality. A tourist comes to a place, looks around, takes and leaves. To 'dwell' somewhere means to put down roots. To 'cultivate' implies nurturing and giving instead of taking. 'Faithfulness' is needed to not give up when the going gets tough.

We asked the Lord to show us how to invest our lives to dwell in the land and to cultivate faithfulness despite the cold response that we had received. It is always easier when others embrace a 'promise' that has been received. Holding on in faith in a place of opposition or ridicule is so much harder.

As a foreigner, my first assignment was to start the long journey of learning the language and culture of this small country. I was raised with English and Japanese and had studied French, Norwegian and German before arriving in the Netherlands. During this time of study, Johan worked as a mechanic at a mission's organization which provided practical help to missionaries.

After finishing my first crash course of the language, we were accepted at a Drug Rehab Centre as house parents to the young people trying to come off of drugs. We also got involved in a local church. After several years, the pastor of that church invited us to join him on staff as youth pastors. A Bible School was connected to the church and Johan took on the responsibility of being the Dean of Students. In later years, I would teach English to the young missionary candidates preparing for their overseas assignment.

Over the next season, it became apparent that something was wrong and that I was unable to have any more children. Years of tests followed. A very diligent gynecologist finally discovered the problem and surgery followed. The following year, a little daughter was born. We named her 'Roechama', which means 'God will show compassion'. A year and a half later, a second son was born and we named him 'Judah' which means 'God is to be praised'.

When Judah was three years old, one morning at the breakfast table, I noticed that Johan's eye was not opened properly. One eye was paralyzed, he could neither fully open it or close it.

Johan had always been extremely fit and healthy. Years earlier he had successfully completed the Dutch Commando Training (Green Beret) and had maintained his level of stamina over the years. We knew immediately that something was wrong.

Our doctor sent him to the University Hospital for further tests. The results came back that there was a tumor in the left hemisphere of the brain that was pinching his optic nerve. Initially the doctors said that it was inoperable and gave Johan about 2 to 3 months to live.

Together with a group of precious friends we poured out our hearts to the Lord. Fear, trepidation, anxiety and hope surged through us. We reminded the Lord of Jozua's healing. We reminded Him of His promise of a fresh outpouring of His Spirit upon the land and how we wanted to be a part of this move of God. This promise was surely for both of us? It would just not be the same to see the fulfilment of that without Johan.

As we prayed, the only answer we seemed to get was that the Holy Spirit reminded us to : 'stay close to the Lord'.

We were desperate. We were often frantic.

One day, during a regular prayer time, the Lord gave us Psalm 23:4 as comfort:

'Even though I walk through the valley of the shadow of death, I will fear no evil for You are with me.'

I could not even imagine what this could mean as the idea of the 'valley of the shadow' terrified me.

As the mother of three young children, 9, 4 and 3 years old,I did not know how I could survive in this foreign land without the support of my strong husband at my side.

Answers did not come but only the comfort of the Lord and His Word: 'stay close to Me'. In the same way that a drowning person grabs on to the rescuer for dear life, my only source of stability was to grab Jesus' outstretched hand.

Several weeks went by where Johan thought that if he did not die from the tumor he would definitely die from the excruciating pain. Finally a neurosurgeon was prepared to try the operation. He encouraged us to write out Johan's funeral ahead of time as he was not sure if Johan would survive the process.

The tug-of-war between hope and despair tore our hearts as we wrote out the funeral preparations. We had seen so many times that the Lord had intervened in our lives. We had seen Him lead and guide us. Could He be trusted now? Could He be trusted beyond the questions, disappointments and fears?

We had a wonderful group of friends who prayed with us as this was a life changing event and we did not have a clear sense of what the outcome would be.

Miracles did take place during the operation. The tumor was non-malignant, but a portion of the brain had to be removed in the process.

It seemed like all would be well.

Hours after the operation, Johan had still not regained consciousness. He had slipped into coma, developed pneumonia and was put on a life support system. Three days later, the epileptic seizures started. The seizures were so violent that the hospital bed with the life support system started to move across the floor in Intensive Care.

I was visiting him at that moment when this happened. The doctors panicked and tried various sedatives to try to calm down his body. When all else failed they put him under anesthesia again. They encouraged me to visit him every day to talk to him as they said that he could still hear my voice.

Each day I went to the Intensive Care to talk to Johan, pray with him, sing to him, read the Bible over him and cry buckets of tears. When the person you love is laying in a bed unresponsive to any outside stimulus it is excruciating.

While Johan was in coma, it was easier to hold on to hope.

Two weeks later, during one of my daily visits, I noticed that Johan's good eye was open again. I had a brief moment of euphoria until I realized that he did not really see me. There was no click of recognition in his eye. I could have been a total stranger, the nurse of even the cleaning lady, but there was not a sense that he knew who I was, Carolyn, his wife.

With each visit now, I had another level of pain that was being added on to my already broken heart. Within days, I realized that he had a very limited level of understanding, his vocabulary was fragmented and his own identity seemed to be lost. His life was still dangling on a very thin thread.

After a six weeks in the hospital, he was discharged and I could take home this familiar stranger. The children were traumatized that their papa didn't know who they were. I was traumatized and overwhelmed to know how to handle our lives. No rehabilitation was given to Johan as the doctors were not certain that he would survive. My heart's cry was: 'Lord help'. I didn't know how to balance the daily needs of our family with a sick husband. The looming questions that flooded my soul revolved around how to parent when my spouse was physically present but mentally unable to interact? How do I regain a sense of the future, when every day was reduced to bare survival? How do I impart hope to my children when my own battle with hopelessness was raging? Was it possible to instill a sense of respect in the children for their father when he continued to forget who they were?

Despite the increased dose of medication, Johan continued to have heavy epileptic seizures. Our lives were reduced to the basic level of mere survival. There were no simple answers or formulas to impart, but the Lord did begin to show a few keys that would move us forward in life.

Having been youth pastors in a large church, I knew that my children should not be my source of comfort or counsel. They had enough to cope with without me, as a Mom, trying to regain my emotional footing at their expense. My children had a need for love, stability, predictability, safety, fun and hope despite the uncertainty of our life circumstances.

I also realized that the children would never learn to honour Johan if I did not treat him with respect and honour, despite my own pain and frustration of not being known or understood.

I needed to open my heart to the Lord's comfort and healing presence so that I could impart hope to the children. Hope, not denial of the pain or disappointment regarding Johan's limitations, but hope based on encountering Jesus in the midst of it all.

It was a fine line of taking the leadership in the family, without being pushy, domineering or a control-freak. I cannot honestly say that I always succeeded, but asking forgiveness opened the opportunity to start over again and again and again.

A prayer began to be formed in my heart:

> *'Lord, I don't know how to do this thing called 'life'. Show me how! Show me how to love when*

there is no response. Show me how to teach the children about You, even when our prayers seemingly remain unanswered. Show me how to create an atmosphere of welcome, kindness, fun and peace in the midst of life that seems more like quick-sand than solid ground.'

Impartation to children is more 'caught' than 'taught, as they were watching my actions more than my words.

I needed to create a daily space to draw freshness in my own spiritual walk with the Lord, in order to have the resources to pass on to the children. I would devour the Psalms. They became my prayer book, they became my comfort, they became my source of hope, they pointed me to the Comforter.

I used Scriptures to be the prayers that I prayed over our lives. I asked the Lord to turn the circumstances into 'gold' in the lives of each of the children. I needed to speak words of life and blessing over my spouse. The 'temptation' I had to deal with was comparing our lives with the lives of other 'whole' families. Once this comparison kicked in, it was so easy to get caught up in the 'I wish' and 'woe is me' cycle of self-pity.

As the days turned into weeks, as the weeks turned into months and as the months began to turn into years, the groan of my heart became louder and louder: 'Lord help'.

Psalm 61:2 'When my heart is overwhelmed, lead me to the Rock that is higher than I.'

> Psalm 62:8 'Trust in the Lord at all times, O people, pour out your heart before Him. God is a refuge for us.'

> Psalm 46:1-2 'God is our refuge and strength. A very present help in times of trouble.'

> Psalm 42:5 'Why are you in despair, O my soul, and why have you become disturbed within me? Hope in God, for I shall again praise Him for the help of His presence.'

These words became the anchor of my soul to keep me from sinking into the swamp of despair.

Letters began to arrive with words of criticism and judgment saying that all these things were happening to us because we did not have enough faith.

I would literally lay these letters before the Lord and pour out my pain, fear and frustration to Him. I didn't know what else to do but to hold on to God's hand in the midst of the storms that were ravaging our lives. Our friends were a source of blessing, our family was far away but supportive, but the idea of having a mentor was so new and unusual. Later, an elderly lady took the time to take me under her wings, but that is a story for later on.

There were those people who suggested that I should institutionalize Johan, divorce him and build up a new life for myself and the children. The argument was that Johan was no longer the person I had married. I knew that this was not the answer.

In desperation, I would pray and ask the Lord for His heart. During one of these times, the Lord reminded me of the four wedding ceremonies that we had had. He very gently reminded me that one of His names is LOVE. He showed me that if my human love was not sufficient, I could appeal to Him for His empowerment to love this new Johan with His love. He reminded me that love is a choice, a verb, an action word. Feelings of love can grow when a choice to love has been made.

The continued violent seizures made it very hard for Johan to learn new things. With each new seizure, he would lose vital skills that had just been acquired. He needed to learn how to use a knife and fork again when eating; he needed to learn how to speak again; he needed to learn how to read and write again; he needed to learn who he was again; he needed to learn who we were again. These were daunting mountains that needed to be scaled.

The Lord began to show me that I could pour out my heart on paper.

> Psalm 56:8-9, 11a 'You have taken account of my wanderings, put my tears in Your bottle, are they not in Your book? This I know that God is for me, in God whose words I praise, in the LORD whose words I praise....In God I have put my trust I shall not be afraid.'

My journals became my place of pouring out my heart and my tears to the Lord. His Word comforted me and taught me that He saw my tears, He valued my wanderings and collected them in His special book of Remembrance. One of His names is El-Roi, the God who sees. It was empowering to know that His eyes were on me. He knew me, He knew my name, He knew my struggles, He knew that I was seeking Him with my whole heart. This was not a journey of a quick fix, but a journey of learning to trust during the dark night of the soul. He showed Himself faithful through words of comfort from His Word. My journals turned into a place of encounter with the Holy Spirit.

One day, a neighbor asked me a challenging question. She wondered if Johan still knew who Jesus was because he could still not remember my name. He had been a youth pastor and Dean of a Bible School and had taught countless people about the redeeming story of God's love, but was any of that knowledge left? With his limited vocabulary it was difficult to know if he still knew who Jesus was.

One day, I gathered enough courage to ask him this simple question: 'Who is Jesus?'

From a place that had nothing to do with his mind, but from spirit to spirit he suddenly said: 'Jesus is the Son of God'.

These words were so comforting, like a cup of cold water in the desert. Even though important information like who I was, who the children were, who he was seemed to be lost, he still had an anchor for his spirit and knew who Jesus was.

This event reminded me of the various Scriptures that tell us that when we receive Jesus as Lord of our lives that the Holy Spirit is given as a seal, as a promise, as a down payment of what is to come. Salvation is not located somewhere in our brain but is a spirit to Spirit encounter with our Creator.

These words ignited a small spark of hope in my heart.

My prayers began to change from being about basic survival from morning to afternoon to asking the Lord for strategy as to how to teach Johan how to speak again. Through my study of Scripture I knew that God gave strategy and blueprints to those who were desperate enough to ask Him, trust Him, to receive from Him.

One of the ideas that came to mind was that an environment of words needed to be created around Johan. Just like a baby learns how to talk when others talk to the child, in the same way, Johan needed to hear words. Reading books out loud became the method. The children loved it when I read out loud to them and Johan would sit with us.

One particular day, I was reading the well-known story of the feeding of the 5000. I had heard it countless times in my childhood and had often read it to my children. The story was about an impossible situation where there were 5000 men, not counting the women and children. This took place in a wilderness where there were no other provisions available. The disciples found a little boy who was willing to offer them his small lunch of 5 barley loaves and 2 fish. The miracle took place when Jesus took the bread, gave thanks and began to break the loaves and fish. There was more than enough to feed the multitude. In fact, there were 12 baskets of food left over.

But this time, as I read, I began to have an inner conversation with the Lord: *'I don't even have bread or fish in my hands anymore. The only thing I have is one crumb. The only thing I have is that I still love You as I do not want to go back to be the person I was before I met You.'*

Even though I continued to read, my hand had formed into a fist, symbolically holding on to the one crumb in the palm of my hand. I suddenly had a sense that the Holy Spirit was asking me to open my fist and to give Him the crumb. My response was: *'Lord, it is so small.'*

As I sat there, I realized that I was talking to the Lord. He never asks if something is small or big. He always asks for my whole heart. At that moment, when I opened my hand, I was saying to the Lord that I did not want to sit in that place of self-pity any longer. It was hard to acknowledge that self-pity had become such a big part of my experience, but the truth was that it felt like we had been 'left behind' in the grand scheme of life. I kept on comparing my life before the operation to what it looked like now. That filled me with a sense of despair and purposelessness. I needed to be honest and ask God to change me at this deep, deep level and restore trust in my heart.

I wanted Him to give us another chapter in our lives. What that would look like, I had no idea. I also had no idea what we could do in life except that I wanted to move forward again.

Around the same time as this occurrence, we met up with Floyd McClung from Youth With A Mission. Before Johan's operation, he would take the Bible School students into Amsterdam to do outreach with the YWAM (an international, interdenominational Christian organization dedicated to train and equip young people) staff and students. Floyd had come to the hospital before the operation to pray with him. This meeting turned out to be the turning point in our lives.

Floyd looked at Johan and said: 'God has kept you alive for a purpose.'

These words were transformational, it felt more like a bolt of lightning. We had been living on the edge of hope. All roads to our past life were gone. Even though Johan still had a very limited ability to communicate, God gave Floyd the ability to see him through His eyes. He went on to suggest that Johan do a Discipleship Training School (this is a six month biblical foundational school with Youth with a Mission) in Amsterdam just by himself. This was quite a challenge as we did not know how much Johan would understand. We also did not know if his recurring epileptic seizures would hinder him. Floyd's mentorship was the encouragement that we needed. He created a place for Johan to grow beyond his limitations.

From a place of desperation to take a new step forward, this invitation was accepted. I would bring Johan to Amsterdam on Sunday and pick him up on Friday afternoon. During the ensuing six months, other parts of Johan's brain began to retain language. His vocabulary and understanding began to increase. The school was dedicated to teach the Bible. God's Word is living and powerful. Little miracles started to happen. Other parts of Johan's brain began to be activated and slowly Johan was beginning to make internal connections with his speech. Although it took years for Johan to learn to read and write again; remember who we were; remember his past; and to relearn some of his technical skills, this time was life-changing.

After the course, a decision was made to redo the DTS, but this time as a family. This gave us courage to take the impossible steps into a very uncertain future.

Before the school started, our youngest son was born. His birth helped 'awaken' in Johan the memory of the other children. We gave him the name Ephraim which means: 'God has made me fruitful in the land of my affliction.'

With a baby, a 6 year old, a 7 year old and a 12 year old, we moved into the YWAM Amsterdam training facility for the school.

During these months, the promise that the Lord had given, years earlier, began to be rekindled. Could it be that now was the time to see the fulfilment? I was delighted with every little ray of hope.

As is often the case, the Lord did not reply directly but began to challenge us to move permanently to the city. He said that most people will not quickly read the Bible but that people would look at our lives. He said that whoever would hear our testimony would know beyond a shadow of a doubt that we would not have survived if the Lord had not helped us. His question was if we were willing for Him to write His story into our lives?

Luckily, we said 'yes'.

This did not mean that life, as we had known it in the past, would return. We would need to receive a new assignment to learn how to 'dwell in the land and to cultivate faithfulness'.

What characterizes these years is the development of a tenacious spirit, 'an-I-won't-quit-mentality' based on the reality that God is still the God of the supernatural. He can still make something out of nothing. He is still able to bring resurrection life into areas where death seems to be reigning.

His promise of many decades ago, had been the staying factor in our lives. Working together with the Holy Spirit had become what the journey looked like. Each day had brought many choices between trust or doubt; between hope or despair; between courage or fear.

In some ways, it would have been nice to have had a quicker, cleaner, less traumatic journey, but, I am also aware that I would have missed the opportunity to learn first-hand more about God's presence, grace and love that has been made manifest in the midst of the journey of suffering. I would have missed the treasures that can only be formed in this 'valley of the shadow'. I would have not had the opportunity to grow deeper roots of trust in the LORD. What others 'see' as wisdom in me was formed and nurtured through these trials of daily seeking Him, daily pouring my heart out to Him, daily choosing not to give up, daily trusting that He was still writing His bigger story into our struggles and into our lives.

Our assignment has been on multiple levels. We have a home of hospitality in the inner city of Amsterdam. It is not only a place to extend the 'welcome of heaven here on earth' to those who the Lord brings our way, but it has also become a place of worship, a sanctuary of prayer, a place of mentoring young people, a place to declare that the Lord is King of Kings and Lord of Lords.

We have invested many years in discipling young people, teaching them and mentoring them through our involvement with YWAM here in Amsterdam and throughout Europe.

Some years ago the Lord challenged me to sit down and write. The little crumb in my hand has matured into 3 books that I have authored and 2 others that I have co-authored. When all that you have is put into His hands, miracles can take place.

POINTS TO CONSIDER

- Our own stories matter. Ask the Holy Spirit to show you His fingerprints upon your life and your story. Sometimes it takes some mental work of remembrance to trace His presence in our lives. The Bible is filled with ordinary human stories that reveal more of how the Lord is present in our everyday.
- God wants to reveal His love to us through the journey that He entrusts to us. It is not always easy to detect His love in His dealings with us. But His Word

assures us that He does love and care for us with an everlasting love. Maybe the prayer is to ask the Holy Spirit to open your eyes to be able to see His love more clearly.

- Your own story of redemption forms a backdrop of what you can share with others. First-hand experience is a valuable asset as you can say with confidence that He is an ever present help in times of trouble when you have been in trouble and He has given deliverance. In a time of difficulty, theory is not enough. You will need an encounter with Him that will mark you forever.
- Revelation 12:11 'They overcame because of the blood of the Lamb, the world of their testimony and they did not love their life even when faced with death.' Each time you share your testimony, you are letting the enemy of your soul know, once again, that he did not win.

V How to build a firm foundation

'We appreciate your mentorship. You never speak from a distance but you added your own personal stories which made it easier to connect and show vulnerability ourselves. This made you so accessible to us.' —A Mentee

'I felt stuck in life and needed someone to give me advice, to pray with me and share her wisdom and experiences with me while coming along side of me. I also wanted someone with life experience, integrity, who had a close walk with the Lord. I wanted someone who had experienced hardships.' —A Mentee

The following Scriptures have become a framework to live by.

Matthew 7:24-27 'Therefore everyone who hears these words of Mine and acts on them, may be compared to a wise man who built his house on

> the rock. And the rain fell, and the floods came, and the winds blew and slammed against that house, and yet it did not fall, for it had been founded on the rock. Everyone who hears these words of Mine and does not act on them, will be like a foolish man who built his house on the sand. The rain fell and the floods came, and the winds blew and slammed against that house, and it fell—great was its fall.'

In this story, Jesus related how each of us is called to be a builder. How we build only becomes visible when the storms of life come, and come they will. The key to building well is to build on a firm foundation, the Rock, an Old Testament reference to God Himself. Listening to what He says in His Word and putting it into practice gives the steadfastness, resilience and tenacity to weather the storms that will come. How we build affects those who we are in relationship with as no one would build a home just for himself in Jesus' day. Even in our day and age, we are aware of the fact that our lives influence those who surround us.

As I have contemplated how I am building in life, I have been challenged by Proverbs 9:1:

> 'Wisdom has built her house, she has built it on seven pillars.'

The question I often ask myself is, what are the pillars that have sustained me on the journey that I have just described? There have been many dark, turbulent years. There have been many moments when it would have seemed more logical to just give up, bury my head in the sand or go my own way and do my own thing.

As I have pondered this, the following reflections have formed these lifestyle pillars that have sustained me over the long journey.

1. Lifestyle of Worship

> '*What I learned is that love is a morphing thing and not static. It is something that grows and is not just thrown in your lap. I also saw that many of the things in our life are the direct result of the choices we make along the way and that we need to take responsibility for them.*' —A Mentee

My whole life is meant to be lived as an act of worship to God (Romans 12:1). During the Reformation a Latin phrase was used that gave good definition to this, Coram Deo, which meant that all of life was to be lived before the presence of the Lord. At the core, worship has to do with what my heart loves, pursues and desires.

In the Great Commandment (Mark 12:30-31) Jesus summarizes the first five books of the Bible by challenging those who asked Him what was the greatest commandment of all. 'You shall love the LORD, your God, with all of your heart, and with all your soul, and with all your mind, and with all your strength. The second is this, you shall love your neighbor as yourself.' There is no greater commandment than these. If I try to love my neighbor first without loving God first, I can easily get into a co-dependent relationship. If I were to try to love myself first without loving God first, I could easily slip into a selfish, narcissistic lifestyle. Loving God with my whole heart, my soul, my mind and my strength frees me to love and value myself as God loves and values me. It also enables me to love others with this same love with no strings attached.

Proverbs 4:23 admonishes: 'Watch over your heart with all diligence for from it flow the springs of life.'

I have had to train myself in this area of what I dwell on, what I give my heart to love. It would have been so easy to live from the place of lack and insufficiency. So many things in our lives were broken and irreparable. But the Holy Spirit wanted to teach me to live from that place of 'living water' flowing from my innermost being, despite the circumstances. He wanted to teach me the lesson of multiplication and abundance in a place that resembled a wilderness. Many stories in the Bible about multiplication occurred in a desolate, barren place. The only answer would be the release of the supernatural when all other resources were not available.

I am not a musician or singer, but all of us have been given a song that we can sing. Setting time aside each day for prayer, Bible reading and meditation (which means to think about what I have read) and writing in my journal helps me cultivate this song in my heart. It also gives the Holy Spirit the opportunity to deal with the wrong attitudes, actions and behavioral patterns that must not go unchecked in my life. This is not a burden or obligation as my core value and identity have nothing to do with maintaining these spiritual practices. These practices are born out of love for Jesus and a longing to get to know Him better.

The following meditation on Psalm 42 maybe gives the best summary of what I mean:

Longing is transformed into loving, when I turn
my heart toward You.
When my soul is parched and thirsty, I will turn my
heart toward You.
Agony of spirit has been my constant companion, yet,
I turn my heart toward You.
Memories of past accomplishments intensify my
yearning to turn my heart toward You.
Despair will not triumph over me, when I turn my
heart toward You.
My heart is filled with homesick-longing, despite this,
I turn my heart toward You.
You surprise me with Your love and kindness, as I
turn my heart toward You.
Your songs greet me during the night watch, if I turn
my heart toward You.
Your melody unlocks my harmony, each time I turn
my heart toward You.
Defeat seems imminent, badgered with shouts: 'why
turn your heart toward Him?'

> *Yet my song will rise, my life will radiate the confidence I have found by turning my heart toward You.*

2 Lifestyle of Gratitude

> *'God is writing the script of our lives. He is writing a new story of redemption.'* —A Mentee

The ability to be thankful is a powerful key to break down the stronghold of self-pity. Self-pity dwells on what is lacking in life and on what should have been or could have been. It sours the ability to see what is present and available in the here and now. Gratitude enables one to refocus one's vision on what is, instead of wishful thinking of what might be. There are some pretty challenging verses regarding thanksgiving, thankfulness and gratitude in the Bible.

> 1 Thessalonians 5:18 'In everything give thanks for this is God's will for you in Christ Jesus.'

When days are 'sunny', gratitude bursts forth like shafts of sunlight. The road seems strewn with droplets of gold, making it easy to acknowledge God's goodness. The mystery of this verse is that the conditions surrounding thankfulness are only captured in the word 'in everything'. But can I really be thankful when the days are dark and gloomy? Can I be thankful when the 'fig tree does not blossom' or when there is 'no cattle in the stall'?

What is the key that Paul wants us to grasp? Could it be that 'thanksgiving' actually changes our focus and perspective? Could it be that the only way to make this a reality is to remind ourselves of who God is?

He is:

'An ever-present help in time of trouble'

'A stronghold against the enemy'

'He is able to make something out of nothing'

'Nothing is impossible with Him'

'He enables me to do all things through Him'

Fear of catastrophe, fear of failure, fear of not belonging, fear of purposelessness paralyzes, making it seemingly impossible to raise the voice of gratitude.

It is in the tension of this mystery that the breakthrough is actually entered into.

It is a confession of 'victory' that is on its way.

It is a confession that God is in control.

It is a confession that the 'LORD is my Shepherd, I shall not want'.

Instead of the position of defeat, He wants us to stand to declare His deliverance even before it becomes visible to us.

What Jesus has accomplished on the cross to redeem us forms the surest foundation for thankfulness. The fact that we have received another day of life is a gift.

I would sometimes practice this with the children after our evening meal. We would go around the table to say what we were thankful for. This exercise was not always greeted with enthusiasm but as we went around the table naming the most mundane things we were grateful for (clean sheets on the bed, clean clothes to put on, etc.) we would inevitably come to the point of expressing our gratitude that we had each other to love. This changed the atmosphere of our conversation together as we realized what a gift we had in each other.

3 Lifestyle of Forgiveness

> '*When you asked for forgiveness on behalf of the organization for what had happened when I was on an assignment, this enabled me to break with the lie that I should have been able to handle this by myself. It touched me deeply that you said that you were proud of me.*' —A Mentee

This has been a hard and challenging pillar to practice. I wanted to name it as a pillar to remind myself that forgiveness is a choice based on the forgiveness that Jesus extended to me when I asked Him to forgive me of my sins. I have been presented with many circumstances that have caused me pain and could have very easily crippled my life if I had not chosen the road less travelled of extending forgiveness, even when the other person did not ask for it. Forgiveness always starts in the heart. It is a choice not to allow the pain and bitterness to take over.

One of these challenges was in regards to the letters we had received condemning us saying that if we had enough faith Johan would not be sick. The Lord said: 'forgive them anyway.'

The first two weeks after Johan's operation, someone called me every day to say that it was my fault that he was sick. The Lord said: 'forgive them any way.'

I had to learn more of what forgiveness actually means. It is not denial that I have been hurt. I had to learn how to name what it was that had hurt me, but then to choose to give the pain to the Lord and release the other person into His hands.

I had to learn not to put my emotional well-being into the hands of other people. I am responsible for my own choices before the Lord. I will have to give an account of what I have done with the grace that the Lord so lavishly gave me. Have I received it? Have I been generous to extend the same grace to others?

Forgiveness also means that I need to learn when I need to ask for forgiveness. For most of the growing up years of the children, I was more like a single Mom. Johan was there, but was often unable to really interact with them or understand them. I overcompensated by trying to be both parents in one.

One day, the Lord challenged me to go to each of my children to ask for forgiveness. For each child, there was something very specific. It was not easy for me to do this as I had tried my best to raise the children to the best of my ability in the midst of very difficult circumstances. The Lord comforted me and said that He knew and saw that I had done what I could, but that there were things that I had done or words that I had spoken that had unintentionally hurt them.

I decided that humility was far better than to be stiff-necked.

The boys quickly patted me on the shoulder and said that they forgave me. My daughter, however, wrote me a seven page letter of all her grievances. I sat down with her and her letter and we went through each point, with tears, words of forgiveness and words of healing.

Looking back, I am eternally grateful for those moments. As the years have gone by, other things have surfaced that needed to be faced, yet again, and worked through, forgiveness and grace asked for and extended. Parenthood is daunting, but when walked in humility, extremely rewarding.

4 Lifestyle of Faith

> *'I admire the way that you follow Jesus and live by faith. I have watched you walk this out over time.'* —A Mentee

Faith is voluntary trust in the Heavenly Father. He has proven Himself to be faithful, just and true, full of compassion, slow to anger and abounding in love and kindness. Each page of the Bible is His love song written for all to read.

The Lord desires that we would know Him.

> Psalm 9:10 'Those who know Your name will put their trust in You.'

Proverbs 18:10 'The name of the Lord is a strong tower, the righteous run into it and is safe.'

Faith has an unshakeable anchor in the Presence of the Lord Himself.

Hebrews 11:1 'Faith is the substance of things hoped for, the evidence of things not seen.'

Hebrews 11:6 'Without faith it is impossible to please Him, for he who comes to God must believe that He is and that He is a rewarder of those who seek Him.'

Faith enables us to soar above the circumstances, as the object of our faith is not grounded in answered prayers, a balanced bank account or thriving relationships but in the One who Promised that His work will not return to Him without it accomplishing that for which He has sent it out.

Faith grows with encounter. Encounter with His Word. Encounter with His ways. Encounter with His presence. These encounters can shape, form and transform the way I see life and think.

Everybody needs a foundation in life that is non-negotiable, something that is as sure and steadfast as gravity.

Daniel 11:32-b says: 'the people who know their God will be strong and take action.' The more we know Him, the more that we know about Him, the more we will be able to put our faith and trust in His reliable character.

5 Lifestyle of Holiness

> *'I learned how simple and powerful repentance is. It was helpful not to get stuck in lies and brokenness and to acknowledge them for what they are and surrender this to the Lord. I needed to let Him fill these places with truth. This is a choice that always can be made despite the circumstances or feelings. It encouraged me to have a steadfast trust in the Lord.'* —A Mentee

When we allow shame and guilt from the past to cause us to hide, we can fall into the trap of living a double life. The Lord wants the inner and outer life to be integrated. Only the Lord knows what is going on in the secret place of each heart.

Hebrews 4:12-13 'For the word of God is living and active and sharper than any two-edged sword and piercing as far as the division of soul and spirit, of both joints and marrow and able to judge the thoughts and intentions of the heart. And there is no creature hidden from His sight but all things are open and laid bare to the eyes of Him with whom we have to do.'

During the many years that Johan still did not know me, I had to really tackle my thought life. I did not want to start to live in an alternative reality of my own making, fantasizing about living another life or with another partner.

I knew that the Lord saw my thoughts and I wanted them to bring Him honour.

> Psalm 86:11 'Teach me Your ways, O Lord; I will walk in Your truth; unite my heart to fear Your name.'

To walk in the fear of the Lord is not from a place of anxiety or from being afraid of Him, but from a place of loving reverence for the Lord, submission to His Lordship over my life and obedience to His Word.

This is rooted and grounded in the unmeasurable love that Jesus has for each of us. He desires that we walk in truth, that we walk in the light and that we walk in wisdom. To live skillfully, we need to have the secret, blind and unknown areas of our heart opened, forgiven, cleansed and restored. I would ask the Lord to examine my heart so that what He saw in my heart of hearts would be pleasing to Him. I asked Him to show me any area where I was deceiving myself or would have the tendency to slip into any addictive behavior to try to medicate my sense of pain and loss. I cried to Him for help. He heard my prayer and set my feet upon the Rock.

Walking in holiness is a daily choice. My prayers from yesterday do not cover my choices today. My prayers from this morning need to be repeated this afternoon.

> Psalm 34:4-7 'I sought the LORD and He heard me and delivered me from all my fears. They looked to Him and were radiant and their faces will never be ashamed. This poor man cried and the LORD heard him and saved him out of all his

troubles. The angel of the LORD encamps all around those who fear Him and delivers them.'

What I focus on will fill my vision, my imagination, my longing, my desire. The fruit of this will be seen in my actions. Nip the thought of sin in the bud. Don't fantasize or dwell on the 'what if' scenarios.

Run to the strong tower. He will deliver when we call out for help.

6 Lifestyle of Prayer

'I am thankful for the prayers and input that helped me reflect on some life issues.' —A Mentee

'I appreciate the prayers and the peace that came. This came through the prompting of the Holy Spirit. I am still in the process of healing but meeting together was a strong catalyst to grow in spite of the pain.' —A Mentee

'What stands out to me is that you pray for the people you mentor. You come with prophetic impressions and you respond when God is prompting you. This has given a significant impact.' —A Mentee

As a parent, I cherish conversation with my children and grandchildren. Nothing brings me greater joy than to share our hearts together. If I as a Mom and Nana have such a strong opinion on communication, how much more does our Heavenly Father long for us to talk with Him. He longs to talk with us as well. He has so many things on His heart that He desires to share with us. He wants me to know how much He loves me. He has plans to prosper me and not to harm me, to give me a future and a hope.

> Psalm 139:17-18 'How precious also are Your thoughts to me, O God! How vast is the sum of them. If I should count them, they would outnumber the sand. When I awake, I am still with You.'

> Psalms 25:12-14 'Who is the man who fears the LORD? He will instruct him in the way he should choose. His soul will abide in prosperity and his descendants will inherit the land. The secret of the LORD is for those who fear Him and He will make them know His covenant.'

The Lord is not afraid of my honest questions, He just wants me not to question His character, integrity and honor.

He communicates, as this is so in line with who He is (John 10:3-4; 27-28).

He communicates through His Word (Psalm 119:105), through an inner prompting that is in line with His written Word and His character (Isaiah 30:21).

There can be visions and dreams that communicate more of what is on His heart (Joel 2:28-29)

He spoke and the world came into existence (Genesis 1).

Throughout our human history He has continued to be a God who speaks. He speaks to build relationship. He speaks so that we will walk in the light. He speaks so that we can learn to recognize His voice.

There are many voices that vie for my attention. It is in the place of abiding in Him that His voice becomes even clearer still (John 15).

As I walk through life with Him, I become even more familiar with His vocabulary, His voice, His ways (Psalm 25:4-5).

His words establish life. His words establish identity. His words establish destiny.

7 Lifestyle of Hope

> *'I would feel God's presence when we would meet together. I knew that you were praying and asking God for guidance in what to share and how to speak into the things that I was wrestling with. My takeaway was that the Holy Spirit would highlight something or confirm something and I would leave with a new or refreshed revelation or insight on something. You gave the encouragement to face my fears in life, to walk in the opposite spirit, repent and bear fruit. You encouraged me to be courageous and speak out*

and stand up for truth. I came away encouraged in my faith and in what I was doing or facing.You encouraged me to carry on. This is hope.'
—A Mentee

Those who have hope will lead. I am not talking about wishful thinking or a false hope built on a flimsy foundation of popular beliefs, but the hope which is anchored in the reliability of the character of God Himself.

> Romans 15:13 'Now may the God of hope fill you with all joy and peace in believing so that you will abound in hope by the power of the Holy Spirit.'

Hope is cultivated by remembering His deeds of the past and His promises for the future. This gives a firm foundation to trust and not fear, whatever may happen, however long it may take.

Over these many years of holding on to the Promise that the Lord gave way back in 1975, I have often reminded the LORD of His promise. As I look back over our lives, this fills me with hope. According to the statistics, we should not have made it to today. But, because of the sustaining presence of Jesus, we have not only survived but are thriving. We were not spared the wilderness years nor the 'valley of the shadow'. There were moments where it felt like this would last forever. But, the LORD has proven Himself faithful.

There is a story in the Old Testament about a man named Caleb that has fascinated me. He was chosen as one of the spies to go on a reconnaissance mission into enemy territory before the Israelites entered the Promised Land. The assignment was to see what sort of land it was; to see what sort of people lived there; to see if it was a fruitful place. The Lord had given the promise that it would be theirs.

Caleb's testimony was: 'we should by all means go up and take possession of it for we will surely overcome it.' (Numbers 13:30)

Except for Joshua, the other spies were intimidated, fearful and not willing to trust in the promise that the Lord had given.

The Lord remarked about Caleb: 'But my servant Caleb, because he has had a different spirit and has followed me fully, I will bring him into the land which he entered and his descendants shall take possession of it.' (Numbers 14:24)

Many years later, in the book of Joshua, we pick up the story of Caleb, after the journey of 40 years in the wilderness, something he had to go through despite his trust in God's promises. He reminds Joshua how he has held onto the promise for 45 years. His resilience and courage is unabated and he is given his inheritance at the age of 85. (Joshua 14:8-14)

We have a strong sense that the move of the Holy Spirit that the Lord promised is about to take place. The years of holding on, despite the storms, has given us deeper roots.

What that will look like in reality, only the Lord knows, but He is looking for a people who will be on the alert, standing firm in faith, ready for action. (1 Corinthians 16:13)

POINTS TO CONSIDER

- How are you building on the foundation of your faith?
- What pillars are you putting into place?
- Hold onto the promises that the Lord has given you, even if there are delays and disappointments.
- Psalm 34: 4-5: 'I sought the LORD and He answered me and delivered me from all my fears. They looked to Him and were radiant and their faces will never be ashamed.'

VI Mentors who have shaped me

Miss Bend

As a little girl, I was shy and afraid of standing out in a crowd or of making a mistake. My temperament made it even harder for me because of where I grew up.

My parents choose to serve as missionaries in post-war Japan. As a nine month old baby, I was transplanted from my place of birth, Seattle, Washington, to Tokyo, Japan. I loved the people and the culture but I did not thrive in the atmosphere of always being different from my Japanese friends and neighbors. With my Nordic looks, blond ringlets and peach colored skin, I stood out wherever I went.

My parents enrolled us in an international school to help prepare us for the transition back to the West after our High School graduation. It is with this as a backdrop that my earliest mentor stands out to me.

Miss Bend taught my fifth and sixth grade class (age 10-11). She had the added challenge of teaching only five of us children making the classroom more of a one-on-one tutoring environment. In order to fill the required hours of education, she came up with an ingenious idea of having us memorize a poem each week and write a short story.

With my vivid imagination, I quickly came up with a weekly story of the adventures of some twins. Even though my facts were not always correct, Miss Bend saw my love for words and encouraged me to explore and to create. She stimulated my imagination, believed in my story line and gave me new vocabulary to create with.

At that time, words like 'being mentored' or 'being a mentor' were not in circulation in my small school in Nagoya, Japan, but Miss Bend personified what this process looked like. She saw something in me that I did not see in myself. She encouraged me not to give up. She gave me tools to work with and fanned the flame of possibilities when I was only thinking in terms of limitations. She shared my efforts with others and thus gave me a tremendous boost in my self-confidence.

POINTS TO CONSIDER

- Be a talent-spotter. They are often the quieter ones in our midst that have deep waters running through their veins. It is easy to notice the class-clown but it takes a special gifting to call forth those who are too shy to come to the forefront.
- Don't wait for failure but give the other person the tools that are needed for success. Miss Bend did this by giving me the educational support that was needed. Maybe one of her greatest gifts to me, as a small child, was her gift of encouragement. She applauded my

effort to create an adventure based on facts that I knew nothing about. For example, I was writing about airplane travel even though I had only travelled the ocean by ship and had never flown before!

- Look beyond the imperfections and imagine what success could look like. Miss Bend made it known that she was proud of me and my childlike effort to create a story. There were other moments that she corrected my spelling and grammar, but in front of the class, she read my story as if it were perfect.

Mr. Burke

By the time I reached High School my parents had moved from Tokyo to Nagoya to Kobe, Japan. Canadian Academy was a much larger international school with 50 kids in my class instead of the 5 that I had been used to. The fledgling confidence encouraged by Miss Bend was still in an embryonic state. Being in a larger class environment also resurrected the timid side of my personality. One particular teacher, however, stands out head and shoulders above the rest.

Mr. Burke's English class made a profound impression upon me. His specialty was public speaking. He would sit at the back of the class to listen to each student's speech. I, however, was terrified of public speaking, but Mr. Burke believed that I had a voice and that my voice needed to be heard.

He would encourage me, coax me and coach me not to give up until my voice could be heard in the back of the room. It takes a certain talent to not humiliate a shy teenager. He persisted and persevered to call forth my voice even before that I knew that I had something to say.

POINTS TO CONSIDER

- It takes a certain conviction to come alongside of someone you are mentoring without being condescending or intimidating.
- Try to understand what the other person is going through. Empathy is putting yourself in someone else's shoes to try to understand them better. As a mentor this is a skill that needs to be developed.
- Without giving a false hope, encourage what you see. Words can have a lasting effect long after the event itself. Discover what words can build up and not tear down. For example: 'I can see that you have put in an enormous effort of time in order to do your work well.' 'Thank you for your courage to not give up.' 'Each time you get up to do something, I notice that you are getting more confident.'
- Don't give up too soon. This applies to being a teacher in a classroom setting, but it is also very valuable as a mentor. Some situations will need more consistent encouragement, correction and direction before change becomes visible.

Patti and Thaddeus

After finishing my education in Japan, I embarked on the long journey back to the United States. Even though I was born there, I had spent nearly all of the ensuing years in Japan. For many young people, the transition from secondary education to the University is also a journey of discovering what you believe about the world, about yourself and about God. Not all beliefs survive this transition. I had been raised with Christian values and beliefs and had embraced many of the precepts but I had not yet had a personal encounter with Jesus.

On my journey from Japan to the US, I travelled through what is now known as Russia, on to Europe to meet my boyfriend. We would then travel to Norway to meet my extended family. On my first day in Europe, we were in a motorcycle accident. I was catapulted over the driver and landed face first in gravel. An ambulance rushed me to the hospital where a dedicated surgeon took hours to remove the small bites of gravel from my face.

As I lay on the operating table I had a life-changing experience. I later understood it to be the Holy Spirit who said: 'Carolyn, don't throw your life away.' I knew that something had to change and somehow I needed to find my way back to God, but I didn't know where to start. It is often a challenge when someone is exposed to the teachings of the Bible without making their own personal commitment to become a follower of Jesus. There was almost a feeling of 'homesickness' that began to grow in my heart to know more about the God that I had grown up with. I felt so very far away from 'home'. After my arrival in the States, I started University and was assigned a dorm room with a roommate. Patti was a vibrant

African-American with a contagious personality and a vibrant commitment to Jesus. Her personal walk with God made me even more aware of what I was missing. she didn't preach to me, but she lived out her faith in a very authentic way. She invited me into her life and introduced me to others who could take me further on my quest.

POINTS TO CONSIDER

- Don't underestimate the power of being an example. St. Francis of Assisi is reported to have said: 'Preach Jesus, and if necessary use words.' Lifestyle is an internal attitude of the heart, this spills out of one's life even when no effort is being made. It has to do with being authentic with no hidden agenda, living one's life before the audience of One.
- Invite others to be a part of your ordinary life as life is a sum total of ordinary days. It is transformational when the supernatural invades our everyday existence.
- It was Thaddeus, however, who went beyond my outward pat answers to help me discover what a real relationship with Jesus is all about. He was aware of the fact that I knew the language of faith but that it had not found a landing strip in my own experience. He helped me explore what the Bible calls confession and repentance.

I needed to acknowledge that I was estranged from God and that my pride and sin could not be bridged by me trying even harder to be 'good'. Maybe one of the hardest steps was facing up to this fact and naming my brokenness and that I really needed Jesus' sacrifice on the cross to save me. Confession is basically agreeing with what God says about something.

1 John 1:9 says: 'If we confess our sin, He is faithful and just to forgive us our sin and to cleanse us from all unrighteousness.'

Repentance is changing one's life-direction, relinquishing control and allowing Jesus to be the center.

To break free from broken patterns in my behavior and mental thought process, I needed to renounce the claim that the devil had on my life through my own choices.

This started me on the journey of replacing the lies that I had believed in with the truth from God's Word.

POINTS TO CONSIDER

- Don't allow intimidation to keep you from asking the hard questions. Be sensitive to the prompting of the Holy Spirit but also ask for wisdom as to what to say and how to say what is needed.
- Ask the Holy Spirit for discernment to understand what is really going on in the life of the other person. What are the lies that are keeping the other person in a spiritual prison? What does God have to say about these things? Encourage the other person to confess their sins before God as you cannot do this for them. James 5:16 gives this framework.

- Tell the truth in love. Sometimes it is not easy to be the bringer of truth, but use words that will communicate love and acceptance. We see this in how Jesus spoke to the woman He met at the well in Samaria (John 4: 7-26). He addressed the issue of her having had five husbands but did it in such a way that healing, forgiveness and transformation followed.
- Be a 'spiritual-midwife'. Jesus spoke about becoming His child in the language of 'being born again' (John 3:1-21). It is such a gift to be able to help someone else find their way home to the loving embrace of the Heavenly Father. (Luke 15).

Maaike

After our two years in Japan, we moved to The Netherlands. I had studied European history and was aware of some of the defining qualities of my new host country. Bicycles, cheese, wooden shoes, dykes, water management, Rembrandt and Van Gogh but I knew next to nothing about their eating habits, the language, the unspoken cultural do's and don'ts.

Our first assignment, upon arrival, was working as house-parents in a Rehabilitation Centre for drug addicts. One of my colleagues, Maaike, was a life saver. She took me under her wings to teach me the Dutch daily routine surrounding when and how to drink coffee and tea. She coached me through the weekly menu of when to eat certain foods and how best to economize and still get the necessary intake of veggies. Growing up in Japan meant that punctuality implied showing up several minutes ahead of the appointed time. Little did I know that in The Netherland being fashionably late denoted a higher societal standing. I was suddenly immersed in a Dutch language only environment. I soon discovered that the words that the recovering drug addicts were using were not to be added to my vocabulary list. Maaike came alongside of me as a mentor to help me navigate this new labyrinth of language and culture. I am forever grateful that she did not see me as a project, but as a friend.

POINTS TO CONSIDER

- Have eyes to see the foreigner in your midst. It goes a long way to help someone integrate into a new country when the people around them respond with patience when the culturally appropriate responses are not understood or followed through on.
- Don't patronize them but help them discover the keys that are needed to be successful.
- When someone is learning a new language, it requires patience on the side of the listener to communicate to them that they can become 'one of us'.
- Recognize the effort that the person is making to get to the level of assimilation that they are at. It is easy to treat a foreigner like a child because their language capability is still so limited. Realize that if they were able to communicate all that they know in their own language, you would have a totally different impression of who the other person is.

- When arriving in a new culture, what is called 'culture shock' will be experienced. Being in a new place may feel like a honeymoon. Everything is different, but inviting. Different but exciting. Different but not threatening. As time goes on and the newness has worn off, frustration may arise at all of the differences and the unfamiliarity of the new culture. Each country has so many 'unspoken rules' that are learned as a child. Moving to a new place as an adult will mean that more time will be needed to understand what these generally understood rules are. After this season, a deep longing or homesickness can arise to go back to what is known and familiar. If the person can persevere and does not give up, they will eventually come to the place of slow acceptance of the new reality as more of the language is learned and understood. The differences that form maybe the biggest area of culture shock are in regards to eating habits, social exchange, time management, language usage, to name but a few areas. If you have the privilege of relating to foreigners, be the bridge to the culture that makes their journey a success story.

Martie

After my husband's operation, I was fighting despair, disappointment, loneliness, bewilderment and many more paralyzing emotions. The life that we had built up together had come crumbling down. I was in a very vulnerable position with very limited encouragement that our circumstances would ever improve or that there would be any hope for the future. In this dark valley, I met a remarkable older woman who gave her time and attention to listen to my hurt and pain. She was a much sought out speaker who had a thriving ministry herself and yet she made time to meet up with me, listen to me and to pray with me. Her investment in my life was transformational.

She encouraged me to remember the promise that the Lord had given to us before we came to The Netherlands. She helped me to address the deeper areas in my heart that needed deliverance and freedom. She was like a lighthouse to me that helped me keep the course without becoming shipwrecked. She never tried to 'fix me' but pointed me to the power of the Holy Spirit to heal, restore and transform me. In my most vulnerable state, she spoke words of destiny and direction into my life.

POINTS TO CONSIDER

- Be available. Never underestimate the deep value of giving your time to someone who is in need. It may seem like a small sacrifice to you, but it can make the world of difference for the other person.
- Be a listener. It takes practice to really listen. To listen without trying to prepare an answer. To listen even if the story is not yet very coherent. To listen to learn about the person, more than their problem.
- Come alongside of the broken-hearted and point them to Jesus. I am forever grateful that Martie saw

me as someone more than the sobbing mess that I was each time I visited her. She saw me behind my tears. She had encountered the Lord herself and knew that pointing me to Jesus was the best advice she could give.

- Know the power of the Holy Spirit to transform. Martie had seen the Lord transform her own life. She was walking in this awareness of the power of the Holy Spirit. It was from this place that she prayed for me.

VII. Biblical examples of mentorship

The stories that are shared give hope and perspective to those who listen and follow. In the light of the stories that we hear, our lives are formed. These stories tell us something about ourselves. They give us the bigger picture of how God works to renew and transform circumstances so that shock waves will be felt through subsequent generations.

God is a multi-generational God. In the Old Testament, He is referred to as the God of Abraham, Isaac and Jacob.

The ancient story of the Hebrew people is not glossed over with impossible success stories of individuals who did the predictable or the expected, but rather real-life human drama is incorporated onto each page. The Bible includes strange and mysterious stories. Ones with high drama, improbable heroes with breath-taking climaxes. From these stories we can learn some valuable steps in how to come alongside someone else in a mentoring relationship.

Jesus as mentor

Throughout the Gospels, we get a glimpse of Jesus' mentoring style. His first priority was to nurture His deep intimate relationship with His Heavenly Father. Through His lifestyle of prayer, He knew who to choose to walk closely with Him on His short earthly journey. (Luke 6:12-17)

We read how Jesus was relational. accessible and available to His disciples. He taught them by using very ordinary and practical down to earth examples that were understandable to those who listened. He also practiced and demonstrated His teachings through His lifestyle. Sometimes His mode of teaching was asking questions (Luke 9:18-20; Matthew 16: 13-20; Matthew 17:24-27) or by using illustrations in parables. (Matthew 13:34-35).

Jesus mentored by loving His disciples despite their outbursts, arguments, unbelief and betrayal. After His resurrection, Jesus pursued Peter to reinstate him in his ministry after he had denied knowing Jesus before the crucifixion.

(Matthew 26:31-35; Mark 14:27-31; Luke 22:31-34; John 13:36-38; Matthew 26:69-75; Mark 14:66-72; John 21:15-17).

Jesus mentored by focusing on the disciples potential instead of their weaknesses. (John 1:40-42; Acts 2:41; Acts 4:13; John 21:15-18).

Jesus mentored by giving opportunities for His disciples to practice what they had learned. (Matthew 10:5-8; Luke 9:1).

Jesus focused on building the individual instead of using the individual to build an empire for Himself. Jesus was interested in making His disciples fishes of men, empowering them to disciple others as they had been discipled. (Matthew 28:18-20; Mark 16:15-18).

Jesus introduced them to the source of His power, the Holy Spirit. (John 14;16-28; Acts 1:1:4-8; Acts 11:26; Acts 17:6).

Jesus mentored by displaying humility, transparency and authenticity. He showed them His humanity. (Hebrews 2:17-18; Hebrews 4:15-16; Hebrews 5:8-9; John 4:6; Matthew 8:24; Mark 11:12; Matthew 9:10; Mark 10:13-16; John 2:13-17; John 11:35; Matthew 26:37-38).

Jesus mentored by praying for His disciples. (Luke 22:31-32; John 17).

Jesus mentored through friendship and calling His disciples friends. He went to weddings and had meals with His disciples. (John 15:13-15; John 2; John 6; John 13; John 21).

Jesus mentored His disciples by making them aware that they were to go and mentor others. (Matthew 28:18-20; 2 Timothy 2:1-2).

POINTS TO CONSIDER

- You mentor from that place of your own personal walk with the Lord. Mentorship is a lifestyle that you invite someone else into.
- Be accessible and available. Time can only be used once. We give our time to what is most important to us.

- Seek a variety of ways to communicate and impart truth. Jesus used very practical examples of the sower and the seed; a conversation about living water while sitting at a well; a story about a father with two sons; a story about a house and its foundation.
- Show genuine care for those you mentor. We often read that Jesus felt compassion for those who came to Him. We cannot fake real love and concern. Our actions do speak louder than words.
- Be someone who sees potential in others. Jesus saw the 'raw diamond' in people. The disciple Simon Peter was a natural leader but needed to go through a transformational process to become one of the key pillars in the early Church. (John 21:15-25)
- Give opportunities to the mentee to pass on what they have learned. Jesus gave His disciples assignments to put into practice what they had learned. (Matthew 10:7-8)
- Be real about your own personal journey. You will need wisdom and discernment to know what to share, how to share it and how much to share. Not everything is relevant for the mentee.
- Pray for those you mentor. The Lord knows the mentee more than you could ever know them. Pray that the blessings of the Lord will rest upon them. Pray for wisdom to know what to say and how to say it. Pray that they will grow to maturity in their walk with the Lord. (Colossians 1:9-14; Ephesians 3:14-21; John 17)
- Mentor through friendship. Come alongside of the mentee and find the things that you have in common.

- Encourage the mentee to reach out to someone else. We read in the story of the Samaritan woman at the well that she went back to her town and spread the news of what Jesus had done for her (John 4:39-42).

Jethro and Moses *(Exodus 18:1-18)*

Moses had the most amazing and miraculous backstory. From his birth onward there was a special calling upon his life. The Pharaoh had ordered a genocide of the Hebrew male infants. Through courage and tenacity of spirit, his mother hid him for three months. When this was no longer possible, she made a wicker basket and set him afloat on the Nile River. Divine intervention led Pharaoh's daughter to find him and enlist his mother to be the wet-nurse until he was weaned. He was then returned to the palace to be raised and educated there.

His mother must have imparted to him the stories of the Hebrew people and the longing for a deliverer to set them free from the captivity of slavery during these early, formative years. As an adult he attempted single-handedly to deliver one of his countrymen by killing the overseer who was beating him. This crime was detected and he fled for his life into the wilderness of Midian.

There he met Jethro, a priest, who gave one of his daughters to be Moses' wife. In Exodus chapter 3, YHWH, the LORD encountered Moses in a burning bush as he was tending his father-in-law's sheep. God gave him the assignment to go back to Egypt and deliver the Hebrew slaves from their captivity. This time, not because of position, strength or talent, but based on the word of the LORD. Through signs and miracles, the miraculous took place. After ten supernatural catastrophes, the Hebrew slaves were permitted to leave under divine protection.

The ensuing journey starting with the Passover Exodus, the parting of the Red Sea, the divine destruction of the pursuing Egyptian army, affirmed Moses' leadership position. In Exodus 18, we read that Jethro joins Moses in the wilderness. In their greeting it is obvious that they have a close relationship together. The ease with which they converse shows that there was mutual care, concern, respect and compassion between them. Jethro noticed that Moses was wearing himself out by trying to single-handedly deal with all of the various issues, complaints and criticism of the people. Moses was leading in a crisis situation but needed some help and guidance. Jethro encouraged Moses to appoint different levels of leadership in order for the needs of the people to be met in smaller groups. Jethro instructed him how to train others. Moses took Jethro's plan to heart and implemented the sub-division of leadership.

POINTS TO CONSIDER

- When a change in behavior needs to be addressed, a relationship of trust, love and mutual commitment is needed. This is built over time. In this story we read that Moses was with Jethro for 40 years before the LORD called him to lead the people from slavery to freedom.

- There needs to be honesty and transparency in order to share what the real issues are. In this father/son-in-law relationship we see that there was mutual trust. Moses was able to share his struggles and Jethro came with a suggestion of how to lead in a healthy way.
- In this story, we see that Jethro is happy to see Moses succeed. Jethro did not claim the plan as his own but wanted to see his son-in-law flourish. As a mentor, we much rejoice in the success of those we mentor.
- Moses was teachable and humble enough to listen to and implement the wise counsel that was given to him. This will be a key in any mentoring relationship. Is the other person open to learn? Is the mentee open for counsel and advice? Is the mentor willing to share and let go, leaving the consequences with the mentee?

Moses and Joshua *(Exodus 17:8-16; Exodus 24:12-14; Exodus 33:9-12; Numbers 13-14; Numbers 27:12-23)*

Joshua was a young man with potential. He loved the Lord and showed unwavering dedication to Him. He was constantly with Moses learning, watching, growing and maturing. He had a teachable spirit. He was bold in the face of opposition and dared to stand his ground when his peers doubted God's promises. His faith enabled him to survive the wilderness experience of forty years, preparing him to take over from Moses when he passed away.

Moses provided opportunity for Joshua to be with him through all of the various trials of leadership.

POINTS TO CONSIDER

- Learn how to recognize potential. In the various stories of mentorship in the Bible, we see that the key was seeing the person who had a teachable heart.
- It takes courage to have faith when others show fear. Come alongside and fan the flame of faith.
- Most preparation for leadership will take place behind the scenes. Encourage the mentee to persevere and serve during the formation, waiting period. Pay attention to your own walk with the Lord.

Naomi and Ruth *(Ruth 1-4)*

This is a gem of a story, told in just 85 verses. It is a domestic account about the plight of two destitute widows and takes place in the history of Israel during the time of the Judges. What characterized this historical period was chaos and social turbulence. In fact the book of Judges ends with a scathing comment: 'In those days there was no king in Israel; everyone did what was right in his own eyes.' (Judges 21:25)

Naomi's backstory was sad and filled with bereavement. During a famine in their hometown of Bethlehem (House of Bread), Elimelech, her husband, took her and their two sons to the fertile mountainous, neighboring region of Moab. Instead of seeking the Lord's guidance, he took matters into his own hands.

Tragedy struck and Elimelech died leaving her widowed with her sons to care for. These young men married local women before tragedy struck again. Both sons died childless, leaving three destitute widows behind.

Naomi had communicated to her daughters-in-law about her God, her people and their history. When she heard that crops were once again being harvested in Bethlehem, she chooses to return there. She cared enough for Orpah and Ruth to encourage them to return to their people and remarry within their own people. It takes courage to consider the welfare of others in the midst of your own devastating sorrow.

Orpah chooses to return to her people and their God, but Ruth clung to Naomi. (Ruth 1:14)

Ruth's response is a powerful confession of faith: 'Do not urge me to leave you or turn back from following you; for where you go, I will go and where you lodge, I will lodge. Your people shall be my people and your God, my God.'

Despite Naomi's deep sorrow, Ruth saw something in her life that she did not want to lose. Naomi's example was so compelling that Ruth was willing to follow her impoverished mother-in-law, to love her, serve her and be loyal to not only her, but she wanted Naomi's God would be her God.

As the story unfolds we see how Ruth serves Naomi by taking on the menial task of gleaning in the fields. The Mosaic law provided for the poor by allowing them to gather what was left along the side of the field after the reapers had passed by.

Naomi and Ruth had a loving, caring relationship. When Naomi discovered that Ruth had 'coincidentally' gleaned in the field of Boaz (a distant relative) she instructs

Ruth how to prepare herself to ask Boaz to be her kinsman redeemer.

The short story starts with a funeral and ends with a wedding. the story begins with a famine, forgotten promises and ends with redemption and the birth of a son who would become King David's grandfather.

This very ordinary story of a very extraordinary young woman is included in the genealogy of Jesus as recorded in Matthew chapter 1.

POINTS TO CONSIDER

- Values are caught more than taught. During a time of crisis what your core values are, will surface. We see that Naomi's faith in God sustained her despite the loss that she suffered. Her trust in God was an example that Ruth wanted to follow.
- Naomi and Ruth had developed a high level of trust and respect in each other and love for each other.
- Do we care enough about the welfare of someone else even if it means that we will need to make a sacrifice?

Samuel and Saul *(1 Samuel 9-16)*

Not all mentoring relationships end successfully. The Bible is honest in telling us not only the stories of victory and success, but also in recounting the stories of heartache and disappointment because of the choices that the mentee makes.

In the unfolding story, we see how the Lord instructed Samuel, the prophet, to anoint Saul as king over the children of Israel.

Saul showed great potential and natural abilities. He was handsome and seemed to be the perfect fit to have as king. His stature and presence would impress the neighboring nations. We even read that he prophesied but never that he called on the Lord himself.

His reign quickly deteriorated due to his lack of character, his lack of love for God or the willingness to obey God's word in the small details. He was more intent on pleasing the wishes of the people than on obeying the word of God brought to him through the prophet Samuel. This cost him his kingship and his kingdom.

POINTS TO CONSIDER

- Mentors can only impart so much into the life of a mentee. The mentee must be willing to allow God to develop their character.
- We read that Samuel mourned Saul and was heart-broken at his disobedience. Mentoring can be heart-breaking. When we open up our hearts to impart love, care and compassion to a mentee, we are vulnerable and can get hurt. Samuel does not try to control, manipulate or change Saul's decision. It was a heart issue between Saul and God and the prophet did not try to meddle.
- As a mentor, we must not get all of our hopes and dreams wrapped up in one person. Everyone is responsible for their own choices and decisions.
- Despite the circumstances, we will be challenged to continue to love the other despite the choices that they make.

Barnabas and Saul (Paul) *(Acts 4:36-37; Acts 9:23-31; Acts 11:19-30; Acts 13; Acts 15:36-39)*

Barnabas was an ideal mentor. He had a very special gift of encouragement.

After Saul's conversation on the road to Damascus, Barnabas sought him out to extend his hand of fellowship to this former persecutor of the Church. Barnabas believed in him when others were still doubtful about his conversion experience. It was risky and took courage for Barnabas to believe in the life-transforming encounter that Saul/Paul had had.

Barnabas gave Paul the opportunity to serve while they were in Antioch.

Barnabas gave Paul the space to become the leader and become more prominent.

At a given point, Paul no longer needed Barnabas as a mentor and he was willing for them to go their separate ways as he acknowledged that his mentorship task was completed.

POINTS TO CONSIDER

- A mentor needs to create an environment of encouragement.
- In order to train future leaders, risks need to be taken. Believe in the mentee.
- Find a place for the other to get involved. See the strengths in the other person and help train him/her by giving opportunities.

- Be secure enough in yourself to be able to make the shift from leader to follower. Allow the mentee to surpass you.
- If you are unwilling to retreat into the shadows, you will not be able to train strong leaders.
- You may be called upon to mentor someone with a very different personality profile. Cultivate the ability to be able to see them for who he or she is, giving what you can and then releasing them to succeed on their own.

Barnabas and Mark *(Acts 12:12,25; Acts 13:5, 13; Acts 15:37-41; 2 Timothy 4:11)*

Mark came from a privileged and godly family and was Barnabas' cousin. Mark was invited to join Paul and Barnabas on their missionary journey. Mark, however, deserted them and did not complete the journey. This led to a division between Barnabas and Paul. On the next missionary journey, Barnabas wanted to take Mark along, despite his previous failure, but Paul strongly disagreed. This led to the parting of their ways. Barnabas, however, continued to invest and believe in Mark. In the long run, this approach paid off.

In Paul's letter to Timothy, we read how Paul remarked that Mark had been very profitable to him in the ministry. Mark went on to write the Gospel in the New Testament named after him.

POINTS TO CONSIDER

- Be committed in your investment in the mentee. This does not mean that you are to turn a blind eye to their mistakes or failure, but that you can encourage them to deal with the deeper issues behind the mistakes and failure.

- Take risks with those who have failed and help them get back on their feet again. We will face criticism when we choose to forgive, invest and take risks despite short-comings.

Priscilla, Aquila and Apollos *(Acts 18)*

Priscilla and Aquila were tentmakers who were skilled in their craft. They offered hospitality to Paul and opened their home for the church in Ephesus to meet.

Apollos, on the other hand, had been highly educated and was filled with zeal but lacked wisdom and experience in his message. He was only aware of the baptism of John the Baptist. He needed mentoring to help him grow in his faith. Priscilla and Aquila took note of his strengths. With a gentle spirit, they took him aside privately to instruct him further in the Gospel. They did not publicly shame him. They knew the Scriptures well enough to instruct him further.

Apollos left their company a far better person and was sent on to Achaia with glowing recommendations.

POINTS TO CONSIDER

- Encourage the progress that you see in the mentee.
- If correction is needed, do it privately, in a loving way and in a Scripturally sound way. Matthew 18:15-20 gives a framework of speaking into someone else's life

when admonishment is needed. Go first to the person in private. Stick to what you have observed yourself and not hearsay from someone else. Don't start off with accusation, but affirm the person even if the message that is given may be difficult to process. The goal is not to shame, nor to cast blame but to correct, to build up and to see the mentee grow. If the private meeting does not bring the desired results, Jesus said to take someone else along as an intermediary.

Paul and Timothy *(Acts 16:1-2; 1 Corinthians 11:1; Philippians 2:19-24; Philippians 4:9; I & II Timothy)*

Timothy was a young man with great potential. He had been raised by a God-fearing mother and grandmother. He was a man of character, integrity and courage. Paul chose him to disciple based on the glowing recommendations of others.

Paul and Timothy developed more of a father-son relationship. Paul encouraged Timothy to follow his example just as he followed Christ. He went on to challenge him to put into practice all that he had learned, received and heard from Paul and to entrust these truths to other reliable, faithful people.

POINTS TO CONSIDER

- The goal of mentorship is to see growth in spiritual depth and character. It is personal and relational not institutional.
- Not all mentoring relationships will develop into a spiritual parenting relationship, as this is not the goal.

But in each step of mentoring, care, attention, empowerment and impartation can be given like a parent would give to a child.

- Be on the alert not to make the relationship into a co-dependent one. We will look at this more in depth when addressing the pitfalls in mentoring.
- Choose wisely who you invest in. Look for a teachable attitude and love for the Lord. Paul encouraged Timothy to guard the good treasure that was entrusted to him by the power of the Holy Spirit.

VIII Biblical framework for mentoring

'Through our talks and the questions that were asked, I learned a lot about myself. I also learned a lot by watching your example. This enabled me to hear God's voice more clearly. It taught me about leadership and what it meant to walk with God during a season of suffering.' —A Mentee

'It is helpful to have someone to process with. I am an internal processor and it is easy for me to get stuck in my head with my own limited perspective. It is healthy to have someone to speak into my different situations and to gain wisdom. It gives the opportunity for lies and unhealthy roots to be uncovered that I don't recognize in myself. I needed a safe place to do this. It is nice and healthy to have outside perspective other than my regular friendships.' —A Mentee

Scripture can be read through many different pairs of glasses. Each time the heart-beat of the Father, Son and

Holy Spirit seeking relationship with us, comes through. We are invited into this union, this dance. Jesus came and dwelt among us to teach us what a loving, trusting relationship with Him could look like.

In 2 Corinthians 1:3-11 Paul gives us a framework of our own participation.

He reminds us that God is the God of all comfort and mercy. As we experience His comfort and mercy in the midst of our own personal journey of suffering, we have a first-hand experience that we can pass on to others.

Paul explains that his own circumstances were so dire that he even despaired of life. In the midst of his own valley, he acknowledged that he wouldn't have made it through the difficulties had it not been for the resurrection power of the Holy Spirit. He reminds himself again of who he has known God to be in his past experiences. He is confident in the unchangeable nature and character of God; who He was, is and will be never changes.

He acknowledges how powerful the prayers of others are, but also how transformational his own worship of the Lord is on his own journey. Worship is anchored in the unchangeable character of the Lord Himself.

God understands us so well that He encourages us to speak to Him in an uncensored way. We are reminded in the Psalms that we can 'pour out our heart to the Lord' (Psalm 62:8). As we direct our prayers to Him, prayers of adoration, thanksgiving, confession and supplication, we will see our journey of suffering turned into spiritual growth instead.

It is from this place of first-hand encounter with the presence of Jesus that we are invited to pass on to others, what has been received.

POINTS TO CONSIDER

- Remind yourself of who God is and what He has done in the past. He is the same yesterday, today and forever.
- Receive His comfort and pass this comfort on to others.
- 'Trust in the LORD with all your heart and lean not on your own understanding. In all your ways acknowledge Him and He will direct your path' Proverbs 3:5-6.
- Change the words and song that you are singing over your own life. Our words are powerful and creative. We either put ourselves in 'bondage' or we can use our words to pave a way to breakthrough. (Proverbs 18:21 'Life and death are in the power of the tongue, and those who love it will eat its fruit.')
- God is able to give beauty instead of ashes, the oil of joy instead of a spirit of mourning and a mantle of praise instead of a spirit of heaviness. (Isaiah 61:3)

IX. How to start

'Outside of the actually things we discussed, I take away mental notes on how to be hospitable, stand your ground in the Spirit and yet to be gentle and patient with people.' —A Mentee

I am often asked the question: 'How do I begin to be a mentor? Where do I start?' The easiest place to start is in your own home. Never underestimate the bridge that can be built through simple hospitality. Hospitality is creating an environment where a person feels welcome and refreshed. This provides an environment where the Holy Spirit can work.

Throughout the Bible, we see that this powerful key of hospitality represents extending heaven's welcome here on earth. This is not about 'entertainment' where 'amusement and enjoyment' are the main focus or is the main emphasis on the 'food and drink' that is being provided. It is not about a 'performance'.

Even with very few resources, hospitality can be provided that is life changing as it is always about the heart and the deeper desire to bless, encourage and build up the other person.

My own journey of discovering this value has been punctuated by some very significant learning moments.

I grew up in a very loving home where hospitality was a lifestyle. I thought that it would be an easy endeavor to implement this in my own home after my husband and I got married. We lived for the first two years near Osaka, Japan. We had the privilege of house-sitting on a University campus. this amazing home had 15 rooms!

My husband and I prayed and decided to invite another young couple from church. It took me about two weeks to get up the nerve to invite them and then another several weeks to prepare the meal. By the time the couple arrived, I was a bundle of nerves. I had started my preparations way too early and my carefully planned meal was slowly reaching the point of being overdone. The evening went well, but I was totally exhausted by the time our guests left.

In this place of despondency I prayed a very bold prayer that I was not even sure that I wanted to Lord to answer: *'Lord, show me what is going on in my heart.'*

The Lord did honor my prayer and slowly began to reveal some key issues that were causing me to be overwhelmed and frazzled. The first area that the Holy Spirit exposed in my heart was in the area of perfectionism. I wanted to be the perfect 'hostess' with the best meal, but I had lost sight of the people we had invited.

Another crack in my foundation was the issue of the 'fear of man'. I wanted to make a good impression, but lost sight of who I was serving in the process. I was caught up in the vicious circle of people-pleasing instead of doing what I was doing to pass on a blessing. I was in the grip of the fear of failure as it had become a performance. I was terrified to fail. I was also my own worst critic, judging my abilities and inabilities harsher than was realistic.

This soul-searching turned into a new prayer that has enabled me to discover the joy of hospitality. *'Lord, change my heart and enable me to see people through Your eyes. Enable me to appreciate and bless them on Your behalf. Take down my walls of perfectionism, fear of man and fear of failure. Enable me to be a conduit of Your presence to others.'*

POINTS TO CONSIDER

- Start with prayer. Ask the Lord who needs encouragement, attention of just a relaxing visit. Choose your words wisely so that you do not create a false expectation or a sense that you are claiming someone or trying to manipulate them.
- Look at your circle of family, friends, neighbors, colleagues, or someone in church and then extend an invitation.
- Start with what feels comfortable to you. It could be a meal, but even to have a tea or coffee together can be significant.
- Don't try to position yourself as a mentor, just extend kindness. This may turn out to be a bigger blessing than what you realize. There is a difference in levels of

involvement in someone else's life. This is just a first step in showing a bit of joy of heaven here on earth.

- If insecurities surface, take the time to work through these issues. The Holy Spirit is a Helper, Teacher, Comforter and Wonderful Counsellor. Work this out in prayer. You also may need to open up to someone to talk and pray through the issues that have surfaced.
- In Psalm 34:8 it says: 'Taste and see that the LORD is good.'
- Sharing a meal together is one of the most powerful expressions of welcome and friendship found in every culture. 'Who I break my bread with' shows who I care about, love and consider to be a part of my social class. Meals are a social event. Eating with someone indicates acceptance, recognition, friendship and forms the groundwork for community. Who we spend our time with gives them importance.
- Could we venture to say that the table forms the biblical framework for relationship and community?
- Looking through the Gospels, we read how Jesus shared countless meals with people. He came to seek and save the lost (Luke 19:10) and he did this through eating with those who society did not deem fit, instead of creating programs, projects or events.

Availability

In our home in Amsterdam, we have often had students come and stay, sometimes for weeks, other times for months. One afternoon, Michaela, who was staying with us, asked me if I would join her and her friend for a cup of tea together. It had been one of those days filled with appointments and meetings and I was tired. I was looking forward to have a few moments to myself before the children came home from school and before I needed to start the dinner prep.

There was an inner tug of war going on. What should I do? Finally, I decided that I could spare a half hour to have tea together. As we sat around the dining-room table we immediately had a good rapport that led to a deeper conversation. One thing led to another. Michaela suddenly asked me to share how I had become a Christian. This immediately sparked a stream of questions from Roelofka.

The half hour turned into several hours of heart to heart conversation. At a certain point, Roelofka asked if she could get to know God as her Father. The prayer time that followed was life-changing. We asked Roelofka to stay for dinner and she ended up spending the night.

Reflecting back on this moment. I realized how easily I could have missed what God wanted to do. Simply to take the time to prayerfully listen, drink a cup of tea, be available and open to the prompting of the Holy Spirit led to a transformed life.

POINTS TO CONSIDER

- Availability is the first step in becoming a mentor. Recently I had a request from someone who asked if she could come by for a chat. What struck me was that she had heard, from others, that I have a heart for young people and that I would probably make time for her. She continued to say that she did not know of any older person in her surroundings that would make time to listen to a young person. I prayed about this request and we were able to meet up for coffee. It turned out to be a one-off meeting, but that was all that she needed. She left with some tools but also a sense of joy that she could tell 'her story' to someone who would listen.

- Be open to the leading of the Holy Spirit in prayer. Develop stereo listening. This is listening to a person while listening to what the Holy Spirit wants to say.
- Ask the Lord to reveal what the deeper questions are.
- Be willing to share a meal even if it is just a simple meal. It is not about impressing someone else but creating a welcoming environment where God can work.

Multiplication *(Matthew 14:13-21; John 6:1-13)*

What has God placed in your hands? As you give this to the Lord, He is able to multiply, creating more than enough out of a not-enough situation.

The story of the feeding of the five thousand is a powerful example of what God can do with what is made available. This story has been a rich source of inspiration in regard to the place of hospitality (host-craft) in my life.

There is a tension between having everything readily available and in that sense, playing it safe, and seeing the need, feeling the compassion from the LORD and actually taking steps of giving what you have to Him.

In this story, Jesus was moved with compassion when He saw the hungry, weary multitude that had been listening to Him for hours. Having a heart of compassion is always the starting point of the release of the supernatural. Jesus was interested in meeting the practical, immediate need. He could have created bread out of nothing, but He chose to use what was available instead.

This story takes place in a desolate, wilderness without any provisions or resources readily available. The hour was late denoting that there was no time left for the multitude to find an alternative solution before darkness would fall.

Instead of despair, the question was 'you feed them'. The disciples were asked what they had. The meagre lunch of a little boy was sufficient for Jesus to start with. Never underestimate small beginnings. Don't despise the seeming inadequacy of what is in your hand.

Jesus gave us an example of how to see the release of the supernatural. He looked to heaven, where there is never lack. He blessed it, acknowledging that the Father is the Giver of all good things. He gave thanks, as gratitude releases the blessing of heaven. Once it was blessed, He broke it, and gave it to the disciples to distribute. With each breaking, more of the supernatural was released. The multitude not only ate and was satisfied, but there were twelve baskets of left-overs gathered up.

How much was needed to feed 5000 men, not counting the women and children? With the blessings, breaking, giving out, there was more than enough.

POINTS TO CONSIDER

- What do you have in your hands? Your time? Your home? Your resources? It takes courage to open your home for others. Our home is cozy, warm and old and it would not be photographed for any Home Decoration magazine, but the feedback I get from those who visit is that they feel welcomed, they sense peace, they feel that they can be themselves. I have had to deal with my own fears of inadequacy, comparison, a sense of lack or the proverbial 'what will people think?' As I have allowed the deeper healing of God's presence in these areas, it has led to being more relaxed, at home in my own space and able to welcome others to join me without making excuses.
- Do you sometimes withhold what you do have out of fear of not having enough for yourself? My greatest example of outrageous generosity was on a missions trip to Albania. We took a team to do some practical work in a far-off mountain village. We had all of the supplies with us plus added necessities for the impoverished mountain community. The mayor took me on a trek to visit the little homestead farms. Each home extended the local hospitality of a glass of sour milk with sugar. After six different visits, we came to the last home for the day. The level of poverty was something I had never seen before. There was literally nothing in the home of this widow and her four children. The children scurried about and left, returning with two small roasted ears of corn. Even through it was not the

harvest season, they had gone into the fields and plucked the little corn cobs and roasted them. The children came in the little hut triumphantly holding the offering with beaming faces. I realized that they were wanting me to eat this love offering from their own meagre resources. I tried to convince the mayor that I appreciated the effort but that I really could not eat their food as it felt like I was taking the food out of the mouth of babes. The mayor turned to me in astonishment and asked if I hadn't read the Bible. I assured him that I had, but he went on to say: 'it is more blessed to give than to receive. Do not withhold the blessing from this widow and her children as no one is too poor that they cannot give something.' Tears streamed down my cheeks as I nibbled on the little cobs realizing what an extravagant gift had just been given to me.

- Are you open to give out of who you are? It is often our own scars that become the medal of honour that we can pass onto others.
- Do you allow your heart to be moved with what moves the heart of Jesus? Compassion in this day and age is a rare commodity. Trying to respond to need from our own resources will be limiting, but allowing our hearts to be moved with what moves the heart of Jesus brings us to receiving His empowerment in each situation.

Seeking guidance in prayer

One day I was asked to host a group of Ugandan intercessors who had come to the Netherlands for a ten day fast and prayer time for this country . My husband and I prayed about this request and sensed that we were to use our limited resources to host the group.

I wrestled with the fact that I only had fifty euro in my purse and I needed to buy some necessities for the family. I presented my dilemma to the Lord and asked Him what I should do. I had two impressions: One was what I should prepare for the meal and the other was how to prepare the table in an elegant way. The phrase came to mind: 'treat them like princesses and princes.'

I set the table for a sit-down meal for 22 people. When the guests arrived and saw how the table was set, they exclaimed: 'We feel like you are treating us like princes and princesses!'

I was thrilled to be affirmed in this step of faith.

When the food was served, again they spoke up and said: 'How did you know that this is our favorite food after we have been fasting?'

I was grinning from ear to ear. The Lord knows how to lead in details.

We closed our meal with a worship song. Instead of just a song, it turned into a time of singing that felt like angels were going back and forth.

It was some days later that I finally realized that somehow we had enough food for the family despite that fact that we had invested our last resources in this special meal. Multiplication took place when we placed what we had into the hands of Jesus.

My mother's words came back to me: 'You can never out give God.'

POINTS TO CONSIDER

- Seek God's direction in prayer.
- Don't let fear dictate what you do.
- Choose to bless. God's heart is for all people. He knows what will minister across cultural, racial and ethnic boundaries.
- Give what you have to the Lord and ask for His multiplication.
- It is always about my heart. Can I trust the Lord? Do I trust Him? Have I given Him my all?

Overview of what is needed for hospitality

H. You need a **heart** that is open to the Lord and to others.

O. Recognize the **opportunities** that present themselves to bless others.

S. Be a good **steward** of the gifts that God has given to serve others.

P. Take time to **pray** and listen to the Lord for His assignment to you.

I. Ask the Lord for wisdom as to how to take **initiative.**

T. What you give your **time** to, shows what you value. Invest wisely.

A. Be **available** and **accessible** to people.

L. **Listen** to the words and to the heart of the person you are mentoring.
I. Do not let busyness interfere with your **intimacy** with the Lord.
T. You will need **tenacity** of spirit to persevere through the highs and lows of welcoming others into your life.
Y. Be **yielded** and open to the leading of the Holy Spirit. This will entail giving Him your time, talents, resources and life.

X. Qualities of a good mentor

'Mentors should offer opportunities for growth. They can give an outside opinion on matters where I am too emotionally involved to see the bigger picture. this person should be a safe person to process with and to share from heart to heart without it being inappropriate or being afraid of gossip. This is very different than talking to a friend.' —A Mentee

'I wanted a mentor with whom I could discuss what was going on in my life, both in the sense of finding solutions and finding a good way to handle leading well. I wanted someone to talk to about how I was personally experiencing things. These were things that I did not feel comfortable discussing with my team of other people as it felt like I would be violating confidentiality if I did.I also wanted someone who could help me find solutions and develop good strategies and not just vent my feelings.' —A Mentee

'You display the power of choice.' —A Mentee

Always remember that all of us stand on level ground at the foot of the cross of the Lord Jesus. Being either a mentor or mentee makes no difference as far as the work of redemption is concerned. With this in mind, a potential mentor needs to have his/her own walk with God. We all need to develop and cultivate our own spiritual root system.

Psalm 1:1-3 gives a good framework of how this can be undertaken.

'How blessed is the man who does not walk in the counsel of the wicked, nor stand in the path of sinners, nor sit in the seat of scoffers. But his delight is in the law of the LORD, and in His law he meditates day and night. He will be like a tree firmly planted by streams of water, which yields fruit in its season, and its' leaf does not wither, and in whatever he does, he prospers.'

The Bible is full of images, metaphors and similes to help us grasp some of its deeper truths. Here we read of a person whose life was so rooted that continual fruitfulness characterized it. Not only that, but his life did not succumb to dryness and its leaves never withered. This short Psalm gives us some valuable clues as to how develop an intimate relationship with God.

Strong roots, like these, do not grow in a day as it takes time and investment. But where do we start? What can we learn from this image? A seed will germinate and take root, when it has a conducive environment. In order for the seed of the Gospel to find its lodging place in our hearts, there are some foundational questions we need to ask ourselves and find the answers in order for growth to take place.

- Can I really trust God? What is He like? I will only entrust my life to someone whom I trust and find to be trustworthy.
- What motivates God to do what He does, anyway? The answer that I find to this question will either make me feel loved or rejected.
- Is God really strong enough to take my anxiety, worries and cares from me? The answer here will lead either to fear or faith.

How I view God's character, motivation and ability will affect how I answer these questions. It will also affect how I live my life, exercise my worship or determine the direction my life should take. From the earliest accounts of the human fall into sin, as recorded in Genesis, these three questions were used by Satan to call into question the reliability of God, His nature and character, His word and His actions. God reveals himself in irrefutable words when He says of Himself that He is gracious, compassionate, slow to anger, abounding in loving kindness, that He is faithful, just and true (Exodus 34:6-7). My faulty understanding of God may need to be readjusted to the plumb line of His revealed word. This revelation of God's character enables me to trust Him and have hope, as hope is based on the reliability of God's character.

The eternal paradigm of God's motivation is captured in John 3:16 where we read: *'For God so loved the world that He gave his only Son...'* His love motivated Him to give His best. This love was deep enough to embrace the agony and suffering of a rebellious world and follow through with the plan of redemption (God gave His Son, Jesus, to die on the cross so that the chasm of separation between Him and me could be bridged). If my life is filled with moments of feeling unloved or rejected, this picture is enough to call my heart back to reality to embrace the truth that I am loved.

If I doubt God's ability to do what He says He is able to do, I will always need a plan B ready to escape to when I don't believe that God will answer my prayers. I will also live a life characterized more by fear than faith. Psalm 55:22 calls to *'Cast your anxiety unto the Lord and he will sustain you'*. I don't need to deny the anxious thoughts of fears, but acknowledge them and entrust them into the strong arms of God.

When I know that the God of the Bible is true to His word, reliable, trustworthy, loving and able, then His words can take root in my heart, causing a sturdy, durable, flourishing tree to grow. This tree draws deeply from the stream of living water that Jesus refers to in John 7. The outpouring of God's Spirit within our innermost being is this vibrant stream we can draw from. The food and nutrients for this resilient spiritual life are found in the meditation on God's Word (law). This process of meditation is taking the Word; pondering on it, applying it, internalizing it, not compromising on it. This will lead to growth, strength and fruitfulness.

We have been given an invitation to come to the source, to put down roots, to become resilient people who can stand despite or in the face of whatever life circumstances come our way.

In verse 1 we see three key words. Sit refers to the position that we take in life. Ephesians 2:6 says that we are seated with Christ in heavenly places. Our identity is steadfast and sure. The first chapter of Ephesians underlines the marvelous identity that we have received when we accept Him as our Lord and Savior. We are chosen, adopted, forgiven, redeemed and given an inheritance. We have a well-spring to draw from. He has a plan and purpose for our lives. Once this anchor of identity is secure, a mentor can reach out to others without trying to find their own significance in the process of mentoring.

Lifestyle matters. In Ephesians 4:1 we are called to walk in a manner worthy of our calling. The chapter continues to say that there needs to be a lifestyle change. The old patterns, behavior and lifestyle needs to be replaced with the new.

We are to learn how to walk in love, walk in the light and to walk in wisdom.

The mentor will need to cultivate their own spiritual discipline of prayer, knowing and believing that God hears and answers prayer. (John 10:27; Jeremiah 33:3; Psalm 37:3-5)

To pass the baton of a healthy spiritual legacy on to others, be like this tree planted by the stream of God's deep unfathomable, unconditional love, grace and mercy.

POINTS TO CONSIDER

- Allow the Holy Spirit access to each area of your heart.
- You cannot bring someone else further than what you have gone yourself.
- Keys will be: prayer, the Word and the power of the Holy Spirit.

IX Skills of a good mentor

'We truly appreciate you as a person. Your insight, relationship with the Lord, leadership, your vulnerability are all characteristics of a good mentor. We appreciate your listening ear and your boldness to challenge us when needed. Your sensitivity to listen to the Holy Spirit was revealed in how kind you spoke.' —A Mentee

'You have a beautiful non-judgmental wisdom and you genuinely see the best for the others in their walk with Jesus.' —A Mentee

'A mentor needs to be sensitive to the Holy Spirit and Spirit inspired questions.' —A Mentee

'Your life experiences are relatable to mine. I trusted that you could speak directly into my struggles with love and compassion without invoking shame.' —A Mentee

A mentor needs to create a hospitable space of trust and confidence for the mentee.

A mentor needs to be able to see the potential in the one coming for mentorship.

Build a track-record of care for other people. Others will soon notice whether you have a genuine love for people, whether you are approachable and available.

Some issues in life can be resolved by using common sense, but when issues of spiritual growth and maturity are being addressed, you will need wisdom that only God Himself can give. In James 1:5 we read: 'If any of you lacks wisdom, let him ask of God, who gives to all generously and without reproach, and it will be given to him.'

God knows and cares about the mentee. He can give the discernment and insight that is needed, to pass on to the mentee, what fits with where they are at on their own spiritual journey. It is not that 'one-size-fits-all' as none of us are a clone of the other.

A mentor needs to own their own story and seek to live an authentic life of holiness, character and integrity. Be vulnerable with your own spiritual journey of faith. But again, you will need wisdom as to what to share, when to share and how much to share. It is important that the time together does not end up a monologue but a dialogue.

Character does matter. Character is the person that you are when no one is around you. Do you walk the talk? The importance of this is in the fact that this produces integrity in your life. Does your life show a proven, consistent Christian walk with God?

When opening the conversation, use questions to help the mentee to know where to start to share. Develop open questions; short questions; questions in line with the precious conversation. If a question is not immediately answered, give space for the mentee to reflect in silence. Don't be afraid of non-verbal pauses.

> *'You work well with questions. You are a good listener. You directed me to a deeper level of my issues and my story.'* —A Mentee

Some suggested questions are as follows:

- How are you doing?
- What have been your highlights from this past week?
- What have you learned?
- Has a certain story or a Bible verse been significant for you this past week?
- What is your view of God?
- How have you experienced Him in your prayer life and Bible reading?
- Are there areas that the Holy Spirit is highlighting where you need to receive forgiveness or extend forgiveness?
- Where are you at on your journey of faith?
- What are some of the areas that you would like to grow in?
- How are your relationships?

- Are there areas that you are wanting to see breakthrough in?
- Are there areas of struggle that you would like to share?
- What are some of the disappointments that you are facing?
- What are some of your joys?
- What are you thankful for as you look back on this past week?
- What are some of the skills that you would like to develop?
- What new understanding have you become aware of in yourself?
- What friendships are you developing that encourage you in the area of honest, vulnerability and accountability?

Allow the Holy Spirit to speak to the mentee. Provide a safe space where the mentee can grow in confidence that they can also hear from the Holy Spirit. Being seen, heard and known are powerful keys to providing this safe space.

Keep in mind that we are not responsible to change anyone, this can only be done through the Holy Spirit.

POINTS TO CONSIDER

- When you first meet up with someone ask about them personally. Ask how they fill their days. Address the issue of why the mentee wants to have a mentor. There may be specific areas that they would like to address. The level of openness and transparency is built over time as report, trust and vulnerability are nurtured.

- Know that the Holy Spirit is the best Counsellor and can give the right questions to ask. I have often been amazed at the questions that come to mind after I have prayed. This makes it difficult to make a list of the most frequently asked questions. Grow in trusting that the Lord will speak when you ask Him for insight.
- Be sensitive to the mentee. It takes courage to ask someone to be your mentor. It takes courage to trust someone else with parts of your story. Handle any information that a mentee shares with care. Be a person who respects confidentiality. When someone is verbalizing some difficult hurts, pains or experiences, listen patiently and try not to respond with shock, surprise or disbelief. Try to discern someone's backstory. Be careful to understand when an issue or conversation goes beyond the scope of your mentorship and there is a need for professional assistance. Know when you are over your head in a certain situation. The most loving thing for the mentee is for you to acknowledge that there are others with a greater expertise that would be far better equipped to help them further.

Be careful not to create a fake confidence as this is not a professional therapy or counselling session. What a mentee shares with you, must stay with you unless the mentee gives you permission to share. At all times, treat the mentee with dignity, respect, compassion and grace.

- Don't try to 'fix' the mentee, but commit the process to the Lord in prayer. Each person is responsible before God for their own spiritual journey.
- Be willing to meet someone where they are at. This will take flexibility and sensitivity. Listen with your heart and listen to their heart.
- Embrace the mentee with care, compassion and commitment for the season that you meet together. Try to set a realistic time framework of meeting together. I have erred in this area in the past by not being specific enough about the length of involvement. The way to set this straight is by apologizing and then to pay attention not to set false expectations on a process in the future. I had a situation where the mentee had an unspoken expectation that I would become their best friend. This was not spoken out until she approached me to tell me how disappointed she was in me. We were able to work this out and parted on good terms but it did give me a reality-check about how important it is to be clear in verbalizing expectations.
- Time is one of our most precious commodities. We only have so much of it and how we use our time shows what we really care about. The mentee will feel love when time is spent to hear their heart.

X Word of caution

Before you mentor others, it is advisable to have had a mentor in your own life. Learn how to walk-the-talk. If you are surrounded with broken relationships, it will be hard to mentor someone else in this area. How we work through our relationship with our own parents affects how we interact in our present and future relationships. This is not about perfection or that there are no issues that need to be addressed, but about taking the first steps that are needed to begin one's own journey of restoration.

- We looked at this earlier, but a mentor must not have a low self-image, as you cannot bring someone else further on their spiritual journey than you have gone yourself. It is important for a mentor to deal with the insecurities and hurts from the past. This give a first-hand framework of knowing God's forgiveness and restoration. In Psalm 86:11 says: 'Teach me Your ways, O LORD; I will walk in Your truth; unite my heart to fear Your name.' Allow the Holy Spirit to the open, secret, blind and unknown areas of the heart. As the light of God's presence enters these broken areas, restoration can take place.

- Mentoring comes with a very important price tag: time. A mentor needs to be willing to know how to be accessible but with a healthy understanding of boundaries. It would be wise to say when you are available and when not.
- A mentor must be vigilant not to abuse authority or to manipulate the mentee. Do not make the mentee dependent upon you. At all times maintain proper boundaries. Make it easy to bring closure to the mentoring relationship. It will help at the start to set a time, length of a session and the frequency of the meetings.
- Confidentiality is a very important key. When someone shares from their heart, they need to know that this information will not be circulated around. There are, however, situations where the issues that surface are greater than what is appropriate for a mentoring relationship. If this is the case, talk to the mentee about which steps need to be taken with whom and if you should be involved or not. Honesty, transparency and compassion must be applied in a situation like this. It could be that someone else's gifting or personality type may be more suited to the mentee.
- A mentor should be interested in the success of each one who is being mentored. The relationship is not to build a clientele or to build one's own reputation or

ministry. The relationship should be based on seeing the mentee grow in their faith.

- Signs of co-dependency can include the following:
  - Unhealthy attachment where the mentor is carrying the burden for the mentees problems or taking responsibility for their actions.
  - Doing more than is required to earn the approval of the mentor/mentee.
  - Trying to cover up or protect others from reaping the consequences of their poor choices.
  - In a co-dependent relationship, the mentor/mentee depends on someone else to create their sense of self-worth.
  - People-pleasing is ignoring your own needs and then getting angry or frustrated when these needs are not met.
  - Pay attention to the need to be needed. This is an unhealthy tendency and can led to burn-out.

POINTS TO CONSIDER

- Which steps are you taking to cultivate your own spiritual root system?
- Are you willing to invest time in someone else?
- Be aware of your motives. Why do you want to mentor someone?
- Never manipulate, control or abuse the authority that has been given in the mentoring relationship. If you notice that the mentee is developing an unhealthy dependency upon you, address it quickly.

- Be careful to maintain healthy boundaries.
- Know what your own capacity is as a mentor. We all go through different seasons in life. When my children were young, mentorship looked very different for me than it does in my present life season. Do not compare your capacity with that of someone else.

XIII. Mentee: where to begin

'I prayed, made a list of potential mentors and then approached you.' —A Mentee

'I am an external processor and need someone to chat with. My mother was surprised that I had already dealt with so many issues. She said that most people in middle-age are confronted with these things. I wanted to be pro-active to seek counsel for my excess baggage.' —A Mentee

'I asked the Lord to guide me to someone and He chose you. I saw you as someone with life experience and who would handle my struggles with integrity. The moment I asked you, you pulled out your agenda and we set a date.' —A Mentee

'I wanted a mentor from the older generation and I had heard good stories about you.' —A Mentee

'You are spiritually older and have a proven, consistent Christian walk with God.' —A Mentee

One of the prerequisites for someone seeking a mentor is for them to desire to see spiritual growth in their own life. We are all responsible for our own spiritual journey, but having someone else speak into our life can be a valuable asset. —A Mentee should be willing to go to the deeper level of asking questions about themselves, God and life in general. Realize that if you are an external processor, speaking your thoughts to someone else can help bring further clarity to your own thinking. If you are an internal processor, allowing someone else to draw you out by asking questions can actually help sort through some of the issues that may keep going around and around in your head.

One cannot learn without a teachable attitude, willingness to learn and vulnerability. Seek out someone who you know to be trustworthy, willing to listen to you and open to the Holy Spirit.

Be aware of what area in your life that you would like a mentor to speak into. Look for someone who has some life experience in that particular area. It is valuable to have someone who has journeyed longer, further and deeper and from that place to be able to speak into your life.

Look for a safe place to process your thoughts, fears, desires and past experiences. Know that you need a safe space to be able to cry, share, feel, express doubt and to experience joy. Choose wisely.

POINTS TO CONSIDER

- Take responsibility for your own journey. Realize that change takes time, energy, dedication and tenacity of spirit. Make sure that you do your own homework as change comes when you put into practice what you have heard. Experience will not change us, but as we evaluate our experiences and learn what to hold on to and what to let go of, change will come.

- Allowing someone to speak into your life during the highs and lows of your journey, is important, but always maintain a healthy boundary.
- Look for someone who is secure in his/her relationship with the Lord.
- Look for someone who will point you to Jesus.
- Look for someone who has a foundation in God's Word.
- Look for someone who will empower you and not try to fix you.
- It will take courage and vulnerability to open up your heart, but there can be healing, redemption and renewal on this journey.

XIV CONCLUSION

'I felt supported and backed up by you. I felt trusted and believed in even in the challenges. I really felt like you never gave up on me.' —A Mentee

'You provided a listening ear. You listened with compassion and spoke words of love, gleaned from your walk with Jesus.' —A Mentee

'I wanted to grow in faith, have someone to share my experiences with and then to be able to pray together.' —A Mentee

'It is valuable to have someone who has journeyed longer, further, deeper and from that place to be able to speak into my life.' —A Mentee

'It is important to have wise counsel from others who have gone before me and have learned many lessons along the way. I think that it is valuable

> *to learn from their experiences and earned insights.'* —A Mentee

> *'You are wise, open, tender-hearted and a safe person to share my heart with. I knew that you would handle what I shared with gentleness but also that you would speak the truth boldly where I needed to hear it. You are not afraid to challenge in a loving way.'* —A Mentee

> *'I knew that I would not be mentored in a shallow way. I knew that you would continually point me to God in everything. You are trustworthy and a very safe person to talk to about deeper struggles without being judged.'* —A Mentee

These brief reflections, from some of my mentees, have given me a deeper understanding of the longing and need for mentorship. There is a desire for someone to be available to come alongside and walk with a mentee for a season.

What I have learned from my mentees is that they were willing to take the step that was needed to approach me. They were proactive on their journey of discipleship. Each of us is responsible for our spiritual growth and these mentees took on this responsibility to ask for assistance.

My question is to the potential mentor: Are you willing to embrace the challenge to become a mentor?

My question is to the potential mentee: Will you be bold enough to ask someone to be your mentor?

In closing I would like to share a story from the culture that I grew up in.

The Japanese are famous for their pottery. There is a special art form that happens when one of the pieces of pottery falls and shatters. The master potter will not throw away the fragmented pieces, but he takes lacquer and powdered gold and painstakingly fits the pieces back together again. In the eyes of the potter, the restored piece is more valuable now, after its' breakage, than before. The repairs actually add value to the restored object. In fact the history of the breakage forms part of the story of the piece of pottery. This art form is known as Kintsugi or Kintsukuroi (gold applied to darkness).

Japanese Christians see this art form as the story of the Gospel hidden within their culture. When Jesus finds us, all of us are broken in one way or another. Some of the pieces seem irreplaceable and irreparable. But the message of Redemption is that in the hands of the Master Potter, Jesus Himself, can take the fragments and make something beautiful out of our mess.

Isaiah 61:1-3 gives us the framework of the mission of Jesus.

'The Spirit of the Lord GOD is upon me because the LORD has anointed me to bring good news to the afflicted; He has sent me to bind up the broken-hearted, to proclaim liberty to captives and freedom to prisoners, to proclaim the favourable year of the LORD and the day of vengeance of our God. To grant those who mourn in Zion, giving them beauty instead of ashes, the oil of joy instead of mourning, the mantle of praise instead of a spirit of fainting. So they will be called oaks of righteousness, the planting of the LORD that He may be glorified.'

In mentorship, we come alongside of a mentee to point them to the Master Potter who is able to restore, redeem, renew and make whole all who come to Him. We are just a signpost.